NASCAR
THEN & NOW

BEN WHITE
Contemporary images by NIGEL KINRADE
Historical images by SMYLE MEDIA

First published in 2010 by Motorbooks, an imprint of MBI Publishing Company, 400 First Avenue North, Suite 400, Minneapolis, MN 55401 USA

Motorbooks titles are also available at discounts in bulk quantity for industrial or sales-promotional use. For details write to Special Sales Manager at MBI Publishing Company, 400 First Avenue North, Suite 400, Minneapolis, MN 55401 USA.

To find out more about our books, visit us online at www.motorbooks.com.

Library of Congress Cataloging-in-Publication Data

White, Ben, 1960–
 NASCAR then and now / Ben White ; photographs Nigel Kinrade.
    p. cm.
 Includes index.
 ISBN 978-0-7603-3814-8 (hb w/ jkt)
 1. Stock car racing–United States–History. 2. NASCAR (Association)–History. I. Title.
GV1029.9.S74W49 2010
796.720973–dc22

2009049813

ISBN-13: 978-0-7603-3814-8

Editor: Jeffrey Zuehlke
Design Manager: John Sticha
Design: Christopher Fayers

Printed in China

On the cover: Top: Martinsville, Virginia—1960: Richard Petty in his famous No. 43 Plymouth on his way to taking the first of his record 15 victories at Martinsville. *RacingOne/Getty Images*. Bottom: Four-time NASCAR Sprint Cup champion Jimmie Johnson at the 2008 Ford 400 at Homestead-Miami Speedway. *Fred Vuich/Sports Illustrated/Getty Images*

On the back cover: Top left: Miss Hurst Golden Shifter Linda Vaughn joins Pete Hamilton in celebrating his victory at the 1970 Daytona 500. Top right: Dale Earnhardt Jr. addresses the NASCAR media. Bottom left: Kasey Kahne celebrates a win in the modern NASCAR manner. Bottom right: Richard Petty tumbles violently during the 1988 Daytona 500, one of the worst crashes of his career. Despite the seriousness of the crash, Petty walked away with only minor injuries.

On the frontispiece: A member of the Unocal Race Stoppers at Daytona, circa 1965.

On the title pages: Top left: Junior Johnson and his wife Flossie (right) in Victory Lane at Darlington Raceway after initially being declared the winner of the 1962 Southern 500. However, after a recheck of scoring, Larry Frank was declared the winner. Bottom left: Dale Earnhardt Jr.'s National Guard team stands at attention for the national anthem during pre-race ceremonies before a 2008 race at Bristol Motor Speedway. Top right: Cars sliding through the north turn at the Daytona Beach and Road Course, circa late-1940s. Bottom right: Michael Waltrip leads the field at the start of the 2008 Budweiser Shootout at Daytona International Speedway.

Contents

Introduction

Although stock car racing had become popular in various parts of the United States by the end of World War II, it was Bill France who officially organized it into a legitimate sport in the late 1940s. The part-time race driver from Washington, D.C., felt that if one set of rules could be honored across the country the sport could be built into something respected by all.

In December 1947, France held a three-day meeting to discuss the future of stock car racing. Attendees included promoters, businessmen, lawyers, mechanics, motorcycle racers, and even a turnip farmer. Each wrote suggestions on napkins as to how the sport should be structured. On Feb. 21, 1948, the proper papers of incorporation were put into place, and the National Association for Stock Car Auto Racing—NASCAR—was born.

Running under primitive rules that left plenty of room for creativity, the first NASCAR season featured cars referred to as "modifieds" competing in 52 exciting races around the southeast. Atlanta native Red Byron was crowned NASCAR's first modified champion.

Carrying the momentum of 1948's success, France looked to do something even better the next season. His goal was to

Harold Brasington (left) and Bill France Sr. (second from right) review plans during the construction of Darlington Raceway in 1950.

NASCAR's dirt track roots: A late-1940s modified race.

create a sport that would truly resonate with fans: What better way to do that than by racing the same cars that fans could buy and own themselves? On June 19, 1949, NASCAR's Strictly Stock division made its debut in Charlotte, North Carolina. Thirteen thousand in attendance watched showroom Fords, Cadillacs, Dodges, and Buicks battle it out on a three-quarter-mile dirt track, with Kansas native Jim Roper taking the winner's trophy in a Cadillac. (Flagged winner Glenn Dunnaway had his 1947 Ford disqualified for being equipped with non-stock leaf-style rear springs. This would not be the last time in NASCAR history that a race result would be overturned after technical inspection.) After eight races in 1949, Byron was crowned NASCAR's first Strictly Stock champion. This was the series that later became known as Grand National, then Winston Cup, and now the Sprint Cup division.

One year later, NASCAR was ushered into the superspeedway era when Harold Brasington built a 1.366-mile-long asphalt oval known as Darlington Raceway. The inaugural 1950 Southern 500, won by Johnny

Mantz in a Plymouth, proved that stock cars could hold up in the Labor Day heat, even though tires were so poor that pit crews ran out of race rubber and had to resort to taking tires off of passenger cars parked in the infield to finish the race.

In addition to Darlington, France continued to sanction races at short tracks across the country. His most prestigious event was held on what was known as the Beach and Road Course, a stretch of Highway A1A that joined the sands of Daytona Beach to form a makeshift oval 4.150 miles long.

In 1959, France opened the 2.5-mile Daytona International Speedway. This was followed by more superspeedways throughout the 1960s, including Atlanta; Charlotte and Rockingham, North Carolina; Dover, Delaware; and Brooklyn, Michigan.

Stars of that era, such as Bobby Allison, Buddy Baker, Richard Petty, Cale Yarborough, and David Pearson helped build the sport through their popularity with the fans and from the headlines they generated throughout the 1970s.

But NASCAR's biggest turning point came in 1971 when R. J. Reynolds Tobacco

Company (RJR) stepped in as the Grand National series title sponsor, renaming NASCAR's top division the Winston Cup Series. Tobacco money brought a new corporate sophistication to stock car racing through marketing efforts and bigger purses and helped grow NASCAR into a more widely recognized national sport.

A surprise snowstorm in February 1979 trapped people in their homes up and down the Eastern seaboard, holding them captive while CBS broadcast its first live flag-to-flag Daytona 500. In the end, the storyline couldn't have been more interesting: While Richard Petty, NASCAR's biggest star, won his sixth of seven career Daytona 500s, race leaders Donnie Allison and Yarborough crashed out of the lead on the final lap. When Bobby Allison came by to offer brother Donnie a ride to the garage, words were exchanged between Yarborough and the Allisons, which led to a sensational fistfight—all broadcast on national television. Talk of the exciting finish lasted for weeks.

In September 1985, RJR created a media buzz through a novel and lucrative incentive program: The company offered a $1 million bonus to any driver who won three of the Winston Cup's big four races—the Daytona 500, Winston 500 (at Talladega Superspeedway), World 600 (at Charlotte Motor Speedway), or Southern 500 (at Darlington)—in the same season. This was a tall order, given NASCAR's tight competition, but Georgian Bill Elliott was up to the challenge, scoring wins at Daytona, Talladega, and Darlington that year. Elliott's incredible feat demanded the attention of many sports editors who could not have cared less about stock cars before.

By this time, drivers such as Dale Earnhardt, Ricky Rudd, Tim Richmond, and Rusty Wallace were making their way into the sport's record books, besting the veterans at their own game every chance they got. Their achievements and colorful personalities contributed to NASCAR's overwhelming popularity in the 1990s, which in turn brought a flood of corporate sponsors to the race teams. The result

The loss of Dale Earnhardt was all the more tragic to NASCAR fans because they felt like they knew the Earnhardt family. Here Dale Sr. celebrates in Victory Lane at Darlington in 1989. On his left (head turned away from the camera) is Earnhardt's third wife, Theresa. His daughter Kelley is standing in front of him, holding her younger sister, Taylor. At right is 15-year-old Dale Jr.

was a level of equal footing never before seen in the sport's history. New stars, such as Jeff Gordon, Ernie Irvan, Mark Martin, Jeff Burton, and Sterling Marlin carried the wave of popularity further. Television coverage moved from cable-based outlets to national networks.

The tragic death of Earnhardt on the last lap of the 2001 Daytona 500 brought NASCAR to the media forefront around the world. Since then, Earnhardt's son, Dale Jr., has become the sport's most popular figure, a household name not only in North America but around the world. Every week, he competes against a field that features the best drivers America has to offer, including Gordon, Martin, Burton, four-time champion Jimmie Johnson, 2004 champion Kurt Busch and his ultra-talented brother Kyle, and many other superstars. NASCAR races are held in state-of-the-art facilities around the country with seating for tens of thousands of spectators, and every race is broadcast into millions of homes around North America.

What Bill France envisioned for stock car racing more than 60 years ago has far surpassed even his greatest expectations.

Above: The rivalry between veteran Dale Earnhardt (No. 3 Chevrolet) and up-and-coming young gun Jeff Gordon (No. 24 Chevrolet) kept fans tuned in every week throughout the 1990s.

Left: Dale Earnhardt Jr. inherited most of his father's fans while attracting many more to the sport all on his own.

Chapter 1
Drivers and Teams

NASCAR drivers then (left) and now (above): Richard Petty, Speedy Thompson, and "Tiger" Tom Pistone dressed in race gear from 50 years ago— open-face helmets, short-sleeve shirts, and blue jeans. Today's drivers wear colorful multilayered fire suits that match their cars' elaborate paint schemes. Shown here are three of the drivers who made up Rick Hendrick's 2009 "superteam": (from left) Jimmie Johnson, Hendrick, Jeff Gordon, and Dale Earnhardt Jr.

Good ol' Boys vs. Today's Drivers

As is the case with any endeavor, image is everything. Part of NASCAR's appeal comes from its storied past, created by the rugged men who battled door handle to door handle each Sunday, often in hastily organized races in open pastures, driving hopped up cars without seatbelts, let alone roll bars or any other safety equipment.

It's no longer a secret that many of these first stock car drivers learned the art of driving fast running moonshine through the North Carolina and Georgia mountains. The skills honed on winding dirt roads would translate well to driving on high-banked speedways such as Daytona and Darlington. Slowly, over time, a sport that was thought by some to be rough and undesirable transformed itself into something more sophisticated and professional. Corporate sponsorship expanded the driver's roles beyond the cockpit into product endorsements and public relations appearances. Yes, image is everything, and a driver's image is crucial to his long-term career. Despite the sport's many changes, NASCAR drivers throughout the decades all share one trait: the talent, skill, and relentless desire to go fast, race hard, and win.

Above: In 2004 NASCAR launched a new championship system, the Chase for the Sprint Cup. After the season's first 26 races, the top 12 points finishers become eligible to compete for the title in the final 10 events. Shown here are the 2008 title contenders: (front row, left to right) Jeff Gordon, Jimmie Johnson, Tony Stewart, Kevin Harvick, Clint Bowyer, Kyle Busch, (back row, left to right) Matt Kenseth, Greg Biffle, Denny Hamlin, Carl Edwards, Dale Earnhardt Jr., and Jeff Burton.

Opposite: By 1965 Ford Motor Company had assembled a Who's Who list of motorsports greats to wheel their Galaxies. Dressed in sharp fire-retardant driver's suits—attire relatively new to the sport at this time—are Dick Hutcherson, A. J. Foyt, Fred Lorenzen, Cale Yarborough, Ned Jarrett, Curtis Turner, and Junior Johnson. On Johnson's left are powerhouse team owners Ralph Moody and John Holman.

Champions: Past and Present

It's the age-old question in racing: Is it the driver, or is it the equipment? History is filled with stories of great drivers who never had the cars to reach the pinnacle of their sport. And there are many examples of so-so drivers who had the luck or the smarts to latch on to a winning team and deliver results that exceeded their talent levels. But the truth is that the greatest drivers almost always end up with the best equipment. Occasionally, it's the driver himself who builds and leads his own winning team. In most cases, it's a matter of their talent attracting bids from the best teams.

Regardless of circumstances, it takes a special blend of talent, skill, determination—and maybe just a bit of luck—to make a champion. And it takes all of these qualities in spades for a driver to earn multiple championships and achieve legendary status. Here are eight of NASCAR's greatest champions from the 1950s to the present.

Richard Petty is known as "The King" for good reason. His 200 wins from 1958 to 1992 are nearly double the total of NASCAR's second-winningest driver. His seven NASCAR championships are matched only by the late Dale Earnhardt. Smiles have always come easily for Petty, and he has reason to smile here after winning the 600-mile event at Charlotte Motor Speedway in May 1975. Today, he remains one of the sport's greatest ambassadors.

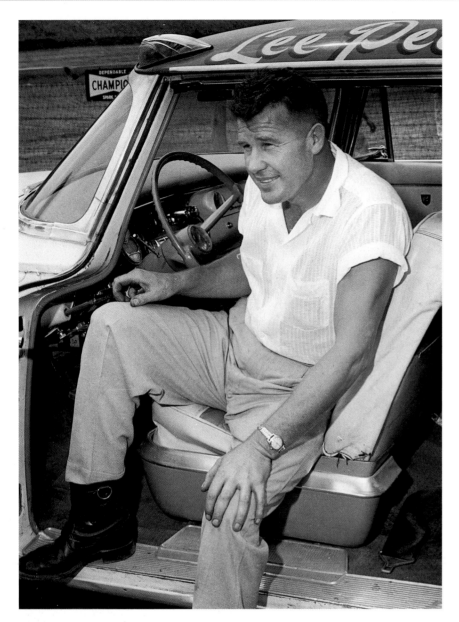

Second only to Petty in career wins with 105, David Pearson was one of NASCAR's most mysterious drivers. During the early stages of a race, he often left everyone—including his crew—wondering how fast his car was, waiting until the final 100 miles of the race to make his move for the win. This strategy earned the three-time champion the nickname "The Silver Fox." The most successful period of Pearson's career came when he collected 43 wins for the famed Wood Brothers team between 1972 and 1979, including 11 wins in just 18 starts in 1973.

Known as the first driver to make a living from racing stock cars, Lee Petty, shown here in 1958, won championships in 1954, 1958, and 1959. He collected 54 wins during a career that began in 1949 and ended with a terrible crash during one of the Daytona 500 qualifying events in 1964. During the years that followed, Petty helped build Petty Enterprises into one of the most successful organizations in NASCAR history with 268 wins and 10 championships.

"Determined" might be the best word to describe Cale Yarborough. He made his unofficial NASCAR debut as a teenager during the inaugural Southern 500 in 1950. He snuck through the fence at Darlington Raceway, jumped into a friend's car, and drove in the race. A NASCAR official caught the underage racer and had him escorted off the premises. The South Carolinian would go on to become one of NASCAR's greatest drivers, notching 83 wins in a 38-year career. His greatest success was winning three consecutive championships in 1976, 1977, and 1978 while driving for Junior Johnson.

Darrell Waltrip (DW) appeared on the NASCAR scene in 1972 as an aggressive and outspoken driver who wasn't afraid to ruffle some feathers. He won his first race in 1975 at Nashville, Tennessee, in his own Chevrolet before becoming a hired driver with many prominent teams. DW collected 84 wins and three NASCAR titles in 1981, 1982, and 1985, before retiring from driving in 2000. He has spent the last decade working in the broadcast booth for Fox and SpeedTV.

Dale Earnhardt's impact on the sport of stock car racing is rivaled only by Richard Petty's. The North Carolina native followed his father, Ralph Earnhardt, into a career in NASCAR, making his first Winston Cup start in 1975. He served notice of his talent by winning Rookie of the Year honors in 1979 and the 1980 NASCAR championship. For the next 20 years, he was the man to beat, earning 76 wins and titles in 1986, 1987, 1990, 1991, 1993, and 1994. Earnhardt's driving style earned him the nickname "The Intimidator," an image enhanced by the solid black paint schemes of his No. 3 Richard Childress Racing Chevrolets.

Born in California, Jeff Gordon entered NASCAR after an incredibly successful career in sprint cars. He made his debut in the second-tier Busch Series (now Nationwide Series), before moving up to NASCAR's elite division in 1992, where he won Rookie of the Year honors. Gordon took his first victory at the Charlotte 600-mile race, beginning a run that currently stands at 82 victories and 4 championships (1995, 1997, 1998, and 2001) through 2009, all with team owner Rick Hendrick. After 18 seasons in the sport, Gordon remains a perennial title contender and one of NASCAR's top drivers.

Since his Busch Series debut in 1998, Jimmie Johnson has quietly built a phenomenal career on par with the sport's greatest legends. After a recommendation from Jeff Gordon, the soft-spoken California native joined Hendrick Motorsports for three events in 2001. Driving full-time for the team in 2002, he was paired with crew chief Chad Knaus, and the two began building a dynasty that has resulted in four consecutive championships in 2006, 2007, 2008, and 2009 . . . and counting.

Crew Chiefs

During NASCAR's early days, the men who called the shots in the shop and on pit road were often referred to as chief mechanics. They usually carried the responsibility of the entire team on their shoulders, including getting the cars to the track and organizing the makeshift, volunteer pit crew into a cohesive unit. After a win, those chief mechanics would occasionally give interviews to radio commentators or beat newspaper reporters.

As NASCAR teams have grown over the years, the jobs within the team have become more and more specialized, to the point that every part on a car is analyzed and repaired only by people with direct knowledge of it. Today's NASCAR Sprint Cup crew chief is often compared to a National Football League head coach. His role is to lead them to make certain that everyone on the team is prepared for every situation on the track. He also "calls the plays" regarding race strategy, and relays the game plan to the driver, the high-speed quarterback who executes the strategy.

With his ever-present cowboy hat, often stained by dirty hands, team owner and chief mechanic Smokey Yunick was an inventor who often applied a perfect mix of science and street smarts to produce race-winning engines and cars. A gruff character who rarely, if ever, delivered his opinions with a sugar coating, Yunick's brilliant mind was constantly coming up with ways to get a leg up on the competition, often stretching—or breaking—NASCAR's rules.

Illinois native Chad Knaus spent the first decade of his career working for several different organizations before being tapped to lead Jimmie Johnson's No. 48 team in 2002. The rest has become NASCAR history, with four straight Sprint Cup championships from 2006 onward. Johnson's skills and smarts, combined with Knaus's technical wizardry and communication skills, have made the No. 48 team the class of NASCAR. When problems arise, the two work their strategy, come back to the front, and often are the ones celebrating in victory lane.

Team Bosses

During NASCAR's early days, "the team owner" was often the same guy who drove the car to the track and ran it in the race. But as the sport grew in the 1950s, it became more professional. By the 1960s many teams had become organized, professional entities, employing drivers, mechanics, engineers, and even marketing and public relations people.

Today, a top NASCAR Sprint Cup team employs as many as 500 people, including dozens of mechanics and engineers, dedicated pit crews, driver coaches, media, licensing, and public relations staff, as well as travel coordinators. NASCAR has indeed become big business, but it is still fueled by the same passion for racing that drove the sport's first competitors.

With nine Sprint Cup championships in his trophy case, Rick Hendrick is the man to beat in today's NASCAR. After a successful career as the owner of race boats, the well-known North Carolina car dealer followed his dream of becoming a NASCAR team owner in 1984. Starting out as a one-car operation with Geoffrey Bodine as his driver, he enjoyed immediate success, and later became a powerhouse after adding Jeff Gordon in 1992, winning four championships with Gordon, the 1996 title with Terry Labonte, and Jimmie Johnson's four championships through 2009.

Opposite: Carl Kiekhaefer was a NASCAR pioneer of sorts, the first team owner to build a multi-car powerhouse team, employing as many as a half-dozen drivers to wheel his solid white Chrysler 300s. A well-known entrepreneur of outboard boat engines, the Wisconsin native was first and foremost a businessman, and the purpose of his brief but dominant foray into NASCAR was to get his Mercury Outboard Motors logos in front of the buying public. He put them in the history books, as well, securing NASCAR championships in 1955 (with Tim Flock) and 1956 (with Buck Baker) before abruptly leaving the sport, citing that he had achieved his goals.

Mechanics and Pit Crews

No professional race team can have success without the support of many people working behind the scenes. Decades ago, a top team consisted of fewer than a dozen people who handled every detail. With sponsorship dollars as little as $100,000 for a single season in the 1970s, the company payroll only had room for essential personnel. There were no fleets of cars filling race shops in the early days of NASCAR racing. At most, a team might build three different cars—one for short tracks, one for superspeedways, and one for road courses.

Today, sponsorships are measured in millions of dollars per season, and shop staffs include not just mechanics, but engineers and technicians, all with specific areas of specialist expertise, whether it is engines, tires, chassis, and many other areas. They all work together in the search for any speed advantage they can find.

In the early years, the front-running Wood Brothers team rarely ran a full schedule, but when they did race, they were always a threat to win, thanks in part to their lightning-fast pit stops. Among the men shown here are owner Glen Wood (far left) and his brother Leonard Wood (third from right), who was known as one of the best crew chiefs and front tire changers in the business. The Wood Brothers team still races today under the direction of Glen's sons, Len and Eddie, and daughter, Kim, with Bill Elliott at the controls of their famous No. 21 Fords.

Dressed handsomely in their colorful flameproof suits, Jeff Gordon's Hendrick Motorsports team members huddle up to prepare mentally for the race ahead. Fast, flawless pit stops are crucial in today's NASCAR. One mistake by any member can make the difference between victory and a dismal finish. This is the reason why the top teams employ dedicated pit crews made up of highly trained athletes who practice daily to shave precious tenths of seconds off of pit stop times.

A Family Affair

NASCAR is a family sport, with roots that run as deep as several generations. This is true not only among the families of fans who have followed the sport since its beginning but also for the sport's competitors. Drivers and teams cherish the fact that their families can come along to wherever they are racing. Wives and children serve as the moral support needed for putting up with the seemingly endless demands that go along with a NASCAR career.

Decades ago, racers were like a band of gypsies, caravanning from track to track in wood-paneled station wagons. Today, racing families congregate with much more style, thanks to large, elaborate motor homes that feature state-of-the-art comfort. Driver's wives and children are always within walking distance of the garage area.

The children of drivers grow up together. They play together, and in many cases, race against one another as they grow older and look to their own careers in the sport.

Ned Jarrett celebrates with his family in victory lane at Darlington Raceway following his win in the 1965 Southern 500. To his left are his daughter, Patti, and wife, Martha. Car-owner Bondy Long is on Martha's left. Lurking somewhere off-camera are Ned's two sons, Dale and Glenn, both of whom grew up to become successful racers themselves.

Top left: Boris Said, girlfriend Deanne Gray, and son Boris Jr. take a break. **Top right:** Sam Hornish Jr. and his wife, Crystal, with daughter Addison behind the wheel of her dad's car. **Above left:** Jeff Gordon is always the subject of an army of cameras, especially when holding his daughter, Ella Sophia. **Above right:** NASCAR champion Darrell Waltrip (second from left) and brother Michael (in driver's uniform) welcome friends and family on pit road.

Fathers and Sons

Few things give a father more pride than to see a son follow in his footsteps. Their youth and optimism bring back memories of a time when they themselves were young and seemingly invincible.

Most sons of racers grow up watching their fathers battle door to door; all the while, they dream of being in the driver's seat themselves. They also dream of the day when the race might come down to a father-son battle for the win.

For a father, watching your son or sons race can be a double-edged sword that can deliver triumph, disappointment, and often both. Every father wants the best for his kids, but any NASCAR veteran knows how easily the disappointments and heartbreaks can come. Above all, fathers hope that their sons or daughters will be safe, as they have suffered injury from time to time and know just how difficult the emotional and physical healing process can be.

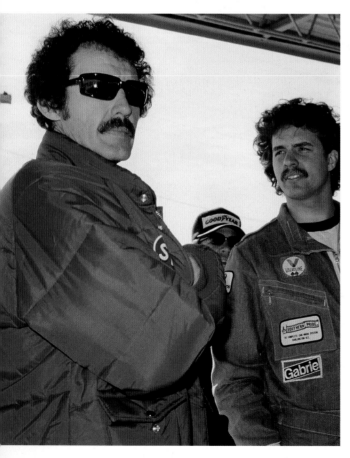

Above: A young Buddy Baker (left) poses for a photo with his father, Buck, in the late 1950s. Buck carried the No. 87 to 46 race wins and championships in 1956 and 1957. Buddy used No. 86 at times and won 17 races during his career, including the 1980 Daytona 500. **Left:** Seven-time NASCAR champion Richard Petty alongside son Kyle just prior to the start of an ARCA event at Daytona in 1979. Kyle went on to win that race, as well as eight NASCAR Sprint Cup events during his career. **Opposite top:** Bobby Allison (center) listens intently to his son Davey, then an ARCA driver, in the garage area during the 1982 season. Six years later, Bobby won over Davey in a one-two finish at the 1988 Daytona 500. **Opposite bottom:** In June 2000, Dale Earnhardt (center) poses for a shot with sons Dale Jr. (left) and Kerry before the start of a NASCAR event at Michigan Speedway.

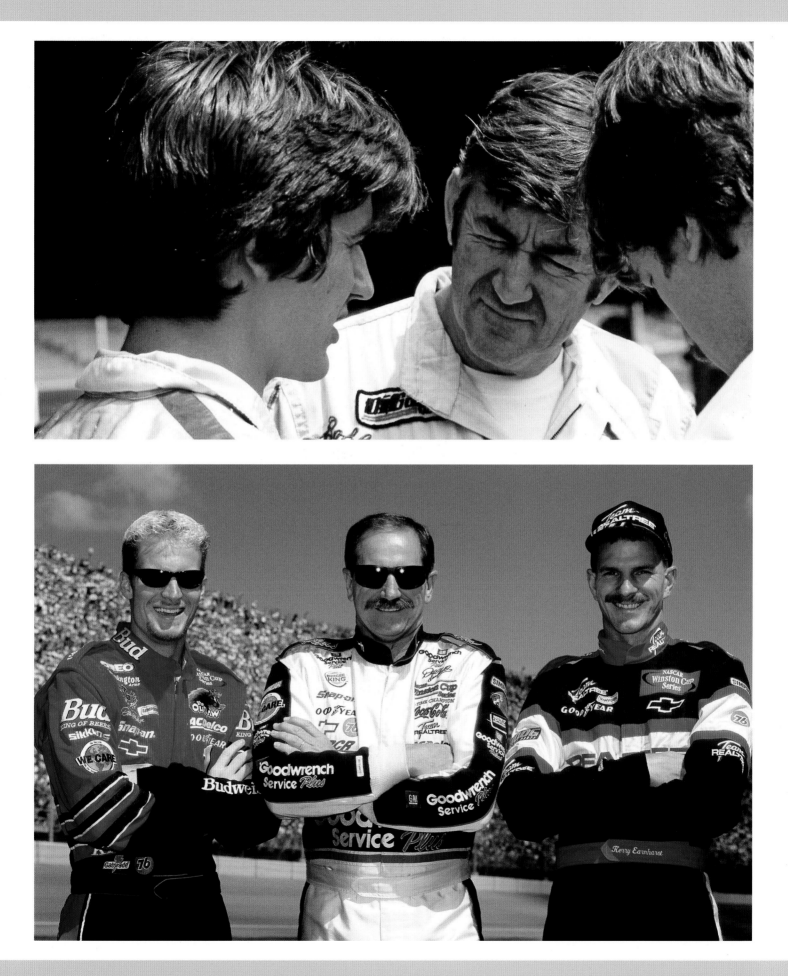

Brothers

Sibling rivalries have been a part of NASCAR from the first official Strictly Stock event on June 19, 1949, in Charlotte, North Carolina. That day, the Flock brothers—Bob, Tim, and Fonty—finished 2nd, 5th, and 32nd, respectively, starting a trend that has continued for more than 60 years. Other sibling rivals have included Bobby and Donnie Allison; Darrell and Michael Waltrip; Rusty, Kenny, and Mike Wallace; Geoff, Brett, and Todd Bodine; and Kurt and Kyle Busch. Most racers will tell you they get a little extra charge out of beating their brothers. After all, siblings are competing with each other in some fashion from day one.

Above: The legendary "Flying Flocks": brothers (left to right) Bob (4 wins), Tim (39 wins), and Fonty (19 wins). The three former moonshine runners from Atlanta came from a very talented gene pool. Their sister, Ethel, was a driver of some note who competed in 100 NASCAR races. Tim won Strictly Stock championships in 1952 and 1955. **Opposite:** Kyle (left) and Kurt Busch take a rare moment from their busy race schedules to talk—possibly about family, but most likely about racing. The two Las Vegas natives grew up racing through the stock car ranks. Big brother Kurt is the 2004 series champion, while Kyle's amazing talents make him a favorite in any race he enters.

Men in Uniform

Back in the day, driver attire was, well, rather primitive compared to today's standards. This shouldn't be a surprise, though. After all, drivers were racing their family vehicles on makeshift racetracks in open fields: Jeans, work pants, and T-shirts seemed to do nicely. Besides, there wasn't much else to choose from, except maybe the standard mechanic's coveralls. But those were hot and cumbersome, especially in the summer. Helmets and goggles—and not very good ones—were the extent of personal safety items.

As the cars became faster and more powerful, the racing became more dangerous. The tragic deaths of several prominent drivers during the 1950s and early 1960s forced NASCAR to demand greater safety measures. Today's drivers wear multi-layer fireproof suits, gloves, and shoes. Full-face helmets and head and neck support (HANS) devices are also mandatory and have combined to make driver injuries and deaths mercifully rare, considering the speeds involved.

Above: Atlanta native Jack Smith sports a typical driver "uniform" from the 1950s: khaki work pants and a flannel shirt. A leather helmet, work goggles, and single roll bar inside his car are the extent of his protective gear.

Left: Clad in blue jeans and a white cotton T-shirt, Jesse James Taylor poses for a picture before qualifying his No. 31 Ford on the famed Darlington Raceway for the second annual Southern 500 in September 1951.

Above: Kevin Harvick makes last-minute adjustments to his full-face helmet just before climbing into his Chevrolet. The multi-layer driver's suit offers protection from fire, while the helmet guards against head and facial injuries. The opening at the top of the helmet connects to a blower inside the car that funnels cool air into the helmet on hot days. **Right:** Dale Earnhardt Jr.'s helmet also carries a fire skirt (in black) that protects the face and neck area. Most modern driver helmets sport special individual paint schemes.

The Driver Lifestyle

Today's top NASCAR drivers enjoy a kind of lifestyle that the older generations probably never even dreamed of. The established Sprint Cup stars earn multi-million-dollar salaries, reside in beautiful mansions, spend race weekends in motor homes that are palaces on wheels, and travel to races in private airplanes.

By the late 1970s, the sport had grown to the point that drivers enjoyed their share of luxuries and conveniences; many drivers of that era collected good salaries, but they did not become rich.

NASCAR's increased popularity in the 1980s brought corporate America into the sport like never before. This translated to more money and more perks for drivers. In addition to their seven-figure salaries, today's top drivers also receive portions of race winnings, bonuses, and money generated through endorsement deals. Any modern driver will tell you he or she owes it all to the generations who built the sport into what it is today.

Above: Richard Petty, daughter Rebecca, and wife Lynda relax in the family's home in Level Cross, North Carolina, in the early 1970s. Petty usually worked in the Petty Enterprises shop during the week and raced for the team on the weekends. Despite his unparalleled success, Petty and his family have always lived a simple, conservative lifestyle.

Left: Paul Goldsmith steps aboard his private airplane in 1966. Goldsmith was one of a handful of racers from his era who owned a pilot's license.

NASCAR drivers spend plenty of time in heavy traffic during the race. One of the many privileges that come with being a top driver is being able to use helicopter transport to travel to and from the track. Here Team Penske drivers Kurt Busch (left) and Sam Hornish Jr. are flying from a sponsor function to Chicagoland Speedway in 2009.

Media Matters

Years ago, the race car driver's responsibilities didn't extend much further than setting up, qualifying, and racing the car. Dealing with the media wasn't much of an issue, because aside from a handful of newspaper, magazine, and radio correspondents, there wasn't much media covering the sport.

As NASCAR has risen in popularity over the decades, the level of media interest has grown along with it. It's reached the point where today's NASCAR driver must be far more than just a wheelman: He is a representative of his sponsor, his team, and his sport. NASCAR's rules mandate that drivers be available to the media at certain set times during the weekend, with failure to do so usually resulting in a hefty fine. Every NASCAR driver understands that the media is what connects them with their fans, that media coverage generates interest in the sport, the kind of interest that has made many drivers multimillionaires. But just about every driver will tell you they feel most at home and comfortable when they are inside their race car where they can focus on what they love to do.

Above: Fred Lorenzen's ability to clearly describe a race made him a favorite among radio commentators in the early 1960s. Many drivers didn't feel comfortable talking to the media and would often shy away from doing interviews. Here the ever-popular Lorenzen describes his pole-winning run at the 1964 Rebel 300 at Darlington. Lorenzen went on to win the race the following day. **Right:** Denny Hamlin, driver of the No. 11 Joe Gibbs Racing Toyota, answers questions amid a crowd of newspaper, TV, and radio reporters. Today's drivers get extensive coaching from their teams to help them understand the best strategies for dealing with the media. For better or worse, drivers learn that saying exactly what is on your mind isn't always the best idea, because controversial comments have a way of coming back to haunt you.

Above: Today, fans can get their NASCAR fix nearly every day of the week, with a number of TV shows that cover the sport from virtually every angle. Here Dale Earnhardt Jr. (far left) and Jeff Gordon (far right) talk racing with the SpeedTV NASCAR Trackside Live team of Elliott Sadler (second from left), Steve Byrnes, Larry McReynolds, and Jeff Hammond. **Left:** With so many print, radio, and TV reporters wanting to interview drivers one on one, NASCAR public relations officials offer press conferences where drivers can address the same or similar questions all at once. Here, Jimmie Johnson of Hendrick Motorsports and Carl Edwards of Roush Fenway Racing answer questions pertaining to their 2008 championship battle.

And Now, Some Words for Our Sponsors

Racing is an expensive sport. Today's bigger NASCAR teams have budgets in the tens of millions of dollars, with much of the funding coming from corporate sponsorship. Their return on investment comes from having their logos displayed on cars racing on national television and by building an association between driver and product to the point where a driver's likeness and endorsement can lead to a purchase at the checkout counter.

In NASCAR's early days, sponsorship was usually limited to a driver or team's local affiliations—restaurants, auto body shops, or lubricants. By the mid-1960s, car dealerships and automotive-related products were often featured. As national exposure grew in the early 1970s, numerous brands joined the NASCAR fraternity, a trend that has continued to this day.

This is Richard Petty lending his familiar voice to a sponsor's radio commercial, circa 1967. Petty may be the King of Stock Car Racing, but this great man doesn't have a snobbish or regal bone in his body. And that's what has made this modest, down-to-earth superstar a sponsor's dream for half a century.

Jeff Gordon addresses a packed crowd of supporters during a pre-race hospitality event. These events offer corporate sponsors a return on their investment by allowing their employees to enjoy up-close access to drivers and team personnel.

Left: For many years, NASCAR celebrated the completion of its season with a banquet in New York City. The event is a sign of how the sport has grown from its Deep South roots into a national—in some ways, international—entity. In December 2008, Jimmie Johnson (left) and crew chief Chad Knaus display their third consecutive championship trophy in New York.

Below: Fox and SpeedTV announcer Mike Joy (left, at podium) emcees the awards ceremony in New York. Although they may not be immediately recognizable without their race suits on, the 12 sharply dressed men on stage are the 2008 Chase for the Sprint Cup contenders: (left to right) Dale Earnhardt Jr., Matt Kenseth, Kyle Busch, Tony Stewart, Denny Hamlin, Jeff Gordon, Jeff Burton, Clint Bowyer, Kevin Harvick, Greg Biffle, Carl Edwards, and Jimmie Johnson.

Meeting the Fans

Throughout its long history, NASCAR has enjoyed a reputation as a fan-friendly sport. As the sport has grown from its regional roots, expanding its fan-base into the tens of millions, Sprint Cup drivers have become celebrities, some of them even household names. And while the fame and fortune are great—especially when you are earning it doing what you love to do—the sheer number of spectators at a NASCAR event requires fences and other crowd-control measures to keep drivers and teams separated from the general public. But today's NASCAR drivers still stay connected to their fans by showing up to offer their autographs in designated areas.

NASCAR star Fred Lorenzen (dressed in white) offers some youngsters an up-close view of his pearl white Holman-Moody Ford Galaxie prior to the start of the 1963 Rebel 300 at Darlington Raceway. One of the most popular drivers of the 1960s, the well-spoken and approachable Lorenzen collected 26-career victories and was the first driver to earn $100,000 in a single season.

Thirty-six years after Lorenzen's impromptu tour, here Kasey Kahne takes some time out of his busy schedule to sign for a throng of fans during a race weekend at Pocono Raceway in 2009. For drivers, there is only one drawback from these autograph sessions: They will often have to replace their uniforms because of accidental marks made on them by all the black permanent markers.

Chapter 2

Fans

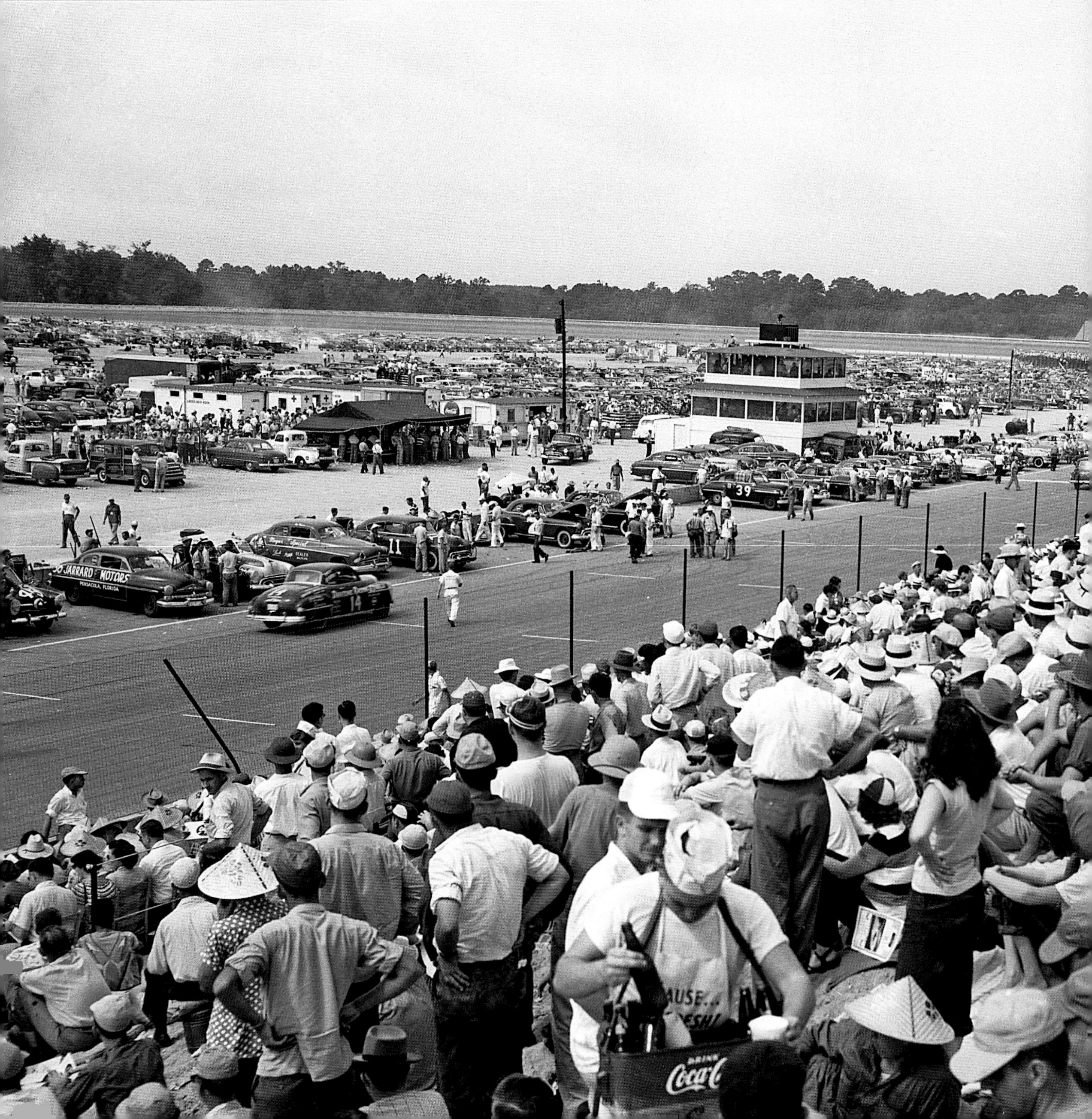

NASCAR fans then (left) and now (above): It's Labor Day 1950, and stock car racing fans from various parts of the country await the start of the first-ever 500-mile race in NASCAR history, the inaugural Southern 500 at the new Darlington Raceway. Compare the attire of the 1950s crowd—including a variety of Fedoras, ball caps, and cone-style Chinese-type headwear (sold outside the track by vendors)—to the apparel worn by fans at the 2008 race at Chicagoland Speedway. Today's crowd sports a wide variety of colorful hats and T-shirts, most of them officially licensed NASCAR merchandise that fans wear to display their unshakable allegiance to their favorite drivers.

Supporting Your Driver

During NASCAR's early days, fan loyalty was more often based on nameplates than on faces and personalities. Those who grew up washing and waxing Chevrolets wouldn't consider having a Ford in the garage, nor would those loyal to Dodge think of having a Pontiac around back. Bill France understood this, and during the sport's early years he catered to these passions with the NASCAR Strictly Stock division.

But times have changed. The variety of automotive choices—both American-made and foreign-built—has watered down some of that brand allegiance. Today, your typical NASCAR fan is more likely to be devoted to a particular driver than the brand of car he drives. The reasons why fans gravitate toward certain drivers are as varied as the personalities of the fans themselves. Some fans like drivers who wear their emotions on their sleeve; others prefer wheelmen who are always cool under pressure. Some may admire the amazing achievements of four-time champs Jeff Gordon and Jimmie Johnson, while others root for the nearly men like Mark Martin and Jeff Burton. Whatever the reason, when fans attend a Sprint Cup race, it's their chance to express their support for their chosen driver. Whether crude or creative (or both), NASCAR fans know how to get their point across—and have fun doing it.

Equipped with only a fitted sheet (possibly from a camper bed) and thick black marker, a fan urges Cale Yarborough to stand on the throttle.

With pit pass in hand and decked out in the sponsorship colors of her favorite driver, this Michael Waltrip fan is standing just outside the garage area at New Hampshire Motor Speedway in July 2007. Waltrip's friendly demeanor and great sense of humor have always made him a fan favorite.

Fans sitting outside the garage area at Indianapolis Motor Speedway convey some personal messages to their favorite drivers.

Show Your Colors

Like fans of any college or professional sport, the NASCAR faithful display their allegiance to their favorite driver or team with officially licensed apparel. The range of products available to the modern fan boggles the mind: from caps, T-shirts, sweatshirts, and jackets to underwear, dog leashes, jewelry, and just about anything else one might imagine. It wasn't always this way. Not until the late 1970s did NASCAR start to take advantage of fan interest by offering its trademark to merchandisers. The result has been a huge industry, bringing in millions of dollars each year to NASCAR, drivers, teams, and sponsors. In return, sporting the colors of their favorite driver allows NASCAR fans to feel a special connection to them.

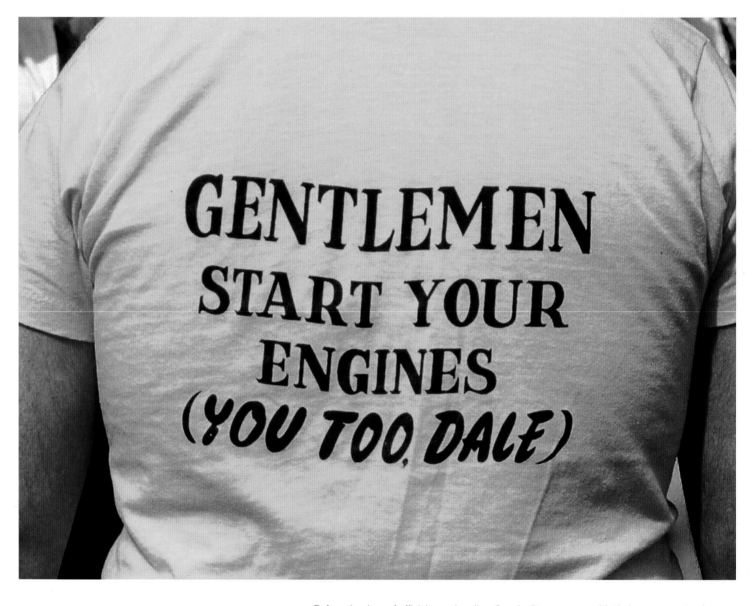

Before the days of official merchandise, fans had to come up with their own ways to show their support—or, in this case, lack of support—for certain drivers. In this picture from the 1980s, a fan is sporting a T-shirt with a few choice words for Dale Earnhardt, whose aggressive style didn't always sit well with some.

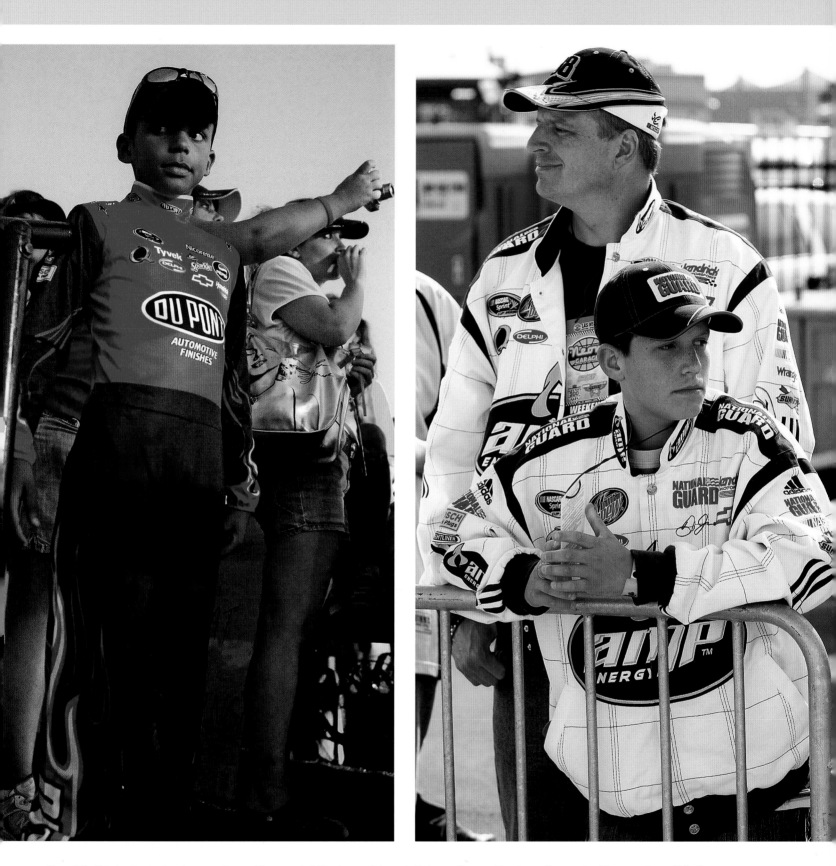

Above left: If imitation is the sincerest form of flattery, Jeff Gordon would surely feel complimented by the outfit worn by this young fan at Talladega Superspeedway in 2008. Today, outfits that resemble drivers' suits are popular with youngsters, many of whom dress up as their favorite driver for Halloween trick or treating. This apparel looks equally at home at the racetrack. **Above right:** When it comes to fan loyalty and merchandising power, no one can match NASCAR's most popular driver, Dale Earnhardt Jr. Here a father and son are sporting their Dale Jr. gear, evidence that driver loyalty is often passed from one generation to another.

Souvenirs and Officially Licensed Products

Before NASCAR began to take full advantage of its licensing opportunities in the late 1970s, handmade trinkets, silk-screen T-shirts, and license plates were often available around racetracks. But the lack of any official licensing agreements meant these items were of inconsistent quality. The fact that NASCAR, the teams, drivers, and sponsors were not earning royalties from such merchandise meant that things would eventually change.

Around this time, NASCAR champion Dale Earnhardt began to explore the idea of licensing his name and likeness to manufacturers. Any merchandising deal he signed included the expectation that the product would be made of top quality material. Through the years, other drivers and teams followed, creating a niche business worth hundreds of millions of dollars each year throughout the 1990s and beyond.

The two photos shown here demonstrate how far the NASCAR merchandising industry has grown in recent decades. Compare how the number of items offered at the entire souvenir stand at Darlington in the late 1970s (left) is matched, if not exceeded, by the number of items dedicated solely to Dale Earnhardt Jr.

Camping Out

Football fans have tailgating, but the NASCAR faithful take the idea several steps further. One of the many benefits of oval-track racing is that it gives fans the opportunity to camp out in the track infield, a tradition that dates back to the earliest days of NASCAR. Forget about trips back and forth to the local hotel: From the camp stoves, sleeping bags, and tents of yesteryear to the luxurious motorhomes of today, there's no better way to make the most of a race weekend than by spending the whole time at the track with thousands of other race fans.

This was a common scene before campers and motorhomes became all the rage. It's the weekend of the 1957 Southern 500, and eight friends have gathered under a tent to pose for the camera. Note the fry pan and coffee pot ready to go on the camp stove.

Left: Sporting a night cap stylish for the times, this race fan probably wasn't expecting anyone to snap a picture of her while she slept away the early morning hours of race day at Darlington in 1968. A couple of pillows and an outstretched tarp are all that's needed for a good night's sleep on the hard steel bed of the family El Camino.

Below: Gray skies above can't dampen the mood of this Dale Earnhardt Jr. fan. Today's motorhomes offer all the comforts and amenities of home, including a restroom, kitchen, comfortable beds, satellite television, and plenty of storage space to haul your memorabilia.

In the Infield

There is nothing quite like watching a NASCAR race from the infield. Not only does it offer fans the freedom to mill around and catch the action from a variety of vantage points, it also creates a sense of being part of a small community. The most dedicated members of the traveling NASCAR caravan usually arrive early in the week in order to stake out the best spots for watching the race. By the time race weekend arrives, the infield is jam-packed with campers and motorhomes, with thousands of fans watching the races, completely surrounded by the greatest background noise in the world: several dozen roaring V-8 engines.

Opposite: Carpentry skills came in handy for this group who showed up in their Hudson Hornet to watch the inaugural run of the Southern 500 in 1950. Such improvisation wouldn't be allowed today on the grounds of safety, but give these fans credit for their ingenuity.

Above: The 2005 Coca-Cola 600 is about to begin at Lowe's Motor Speedway, and fans in the packed infield are settling in to watch the weekend's main event. In addition to motorhomes large and small, several converted school buses can be seen, each equipped with railings on the roof that allow a few dozen spectators to safely watch the race from high above ground. The ingenuity continues.

In the Bleachers

To truly experience the excitement of NASCAR racing, you have to attend an event. Listening to a race on the radio or watching one on television only conveys a fraction of the overall sensation of 43 800-horsepower cars battling it out for 500 miles at speeds approaching 200 miles per hour. Add in the energy created by tens of thousands of screaming fans, and you'll understand why the bleachers are an exciting place to be on race weekend. And seeing a close finish in person, especially in high-profile events such as the Daytona 500 in Florida or the Brickyard 400 at Indianapolis, leaves lasting memories and a sense of being a part of history: "I was there when that happened."

Modern NASCAR tracks feature aluminum bleacher-style seats with fiberglass backs. Not exactly luxurious, but much more comfortable than the bleachers from decades past. Most of the newer NASCAR tracks seat more than 100,000 people. This is Michigan Speedway in June 2008. The crowd shown here is just a fraction of the 160,000 people who attended the race.

Inset: Early NASCAR bleachers weren't particularly comfortable. These fans are sitting in the freshly laid concrete grandstands at Darlington in 1950. Spectators who had the foresight to bring cushions to sit on were certainly glad to have them by the end of the six-hour race.

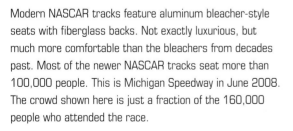

Chasing Autographs

Patience, diligence, and a comfortable pair of shoes are all keys to securing the autograph of a favorite driver. When a NASCAR star passes by, it's usually a quick visit as the driver walks from the garage to the transporter or motorhome. The autograph hunter needs to have pen and items handy to get an autograph at a moment's notice.

Driver Richie Panch signing autographs for fans at Charlotte Motor Speedway, c. 1975.

Above left: Kyle Busch takes a hat from a fan as others slide items through the fence for him to autograph at Las Vegas in 2008. **Above right:** Fans lined up for autographs outside the JR Motorsports souvenir trailer during a race weekend at Michigan. **Left:** Jeff Gordon signs a cast to the delight of one of his fans. **Below:** Even security fences don't discourage fans from getting the best shot possible of their favorite wheelman.

Chapter 3
Horsepower

NASCAR race cars then (above) and now (opposite): Gayle Warren (No. 4 Studebaker) battles with Freddie Farmer (No. 51 Nash) during the 1951 Southern 500 at Darlington Raceway. The era's Strictly Stock cars came right out of family driveways with few modifications. Note the difference in size and shape between the two cars. Today's Sprint Cup machines are virtually identical and must strictly adhere to rigid NASCAR rules. The so-called NASCAR Car of Today, introduced in 2007, was created by the sanctioning body, and to keep the teams from modifying the cars to steal an advantage over rivals, the cars must fit more than 160 body templates. Here Carl Edwards (No. 99 Ford) runs slightly ahead of Jeff Burton (No. 31 Chevrolet), Reed Sorenson (No. 43 Dodge), and Sam Hornish (No. 77 Dodge) at Dover International Raceway in May 2009.

Stock Cars through the Decades

The concept of stock car racing was born in the mid-1940s, in part by former World War II servicemen who were anxious to find excitement in everyday life. Long before Bill France Sr. officially formed NASCAR, drivers were holding races to determine whose Hudson Hornet or Packard could outrun whose Ford or Chevrolet.

As the sport grew from the dirt tracks to the speedways, increased speeds brought the need for safety innovations. The Strictly Stock cars of the 1950s were no longer viable, and by the 1960s NASCAR Grand National machines were really "stock cars" in name only. They were built just for racing, with floorpans and bodies built around extensive roll cages that spider-webbed throughout the car from front to back. Since then, the basic chassis configuration has been used for many decades, with safety innovations being tested and applied along the way. Today's stock cars bear little resemblance to the vehicles they represent in dealer showrooms, but they are designed to provide the high-speed thrills NASCAR fans expect while protecting drivers from the dangers of 200-mile-per-hour competition.

Walt Crawford's No. 64 (1950 Buick) leads Wally Campbell's No. 33 (1950 Oldsmobile), Bob Smith's No. 35 (1950 Oldsmobile), Jack Yardley's No. 54 (1950 Ford), an unknown driver's No. 65 (1950 Ford), and Harold Kite's No. 21 (1949 Lincoln) down the front stretch at Darlington Raceway during the 1950 Southern 500. Most brands were allowed to compete during the early years of NASCAR, as long as minimal safety requirements were met. The cars of the era were numbered with shoe polish by the local sign painter. Note the license plate on the bumper of Crawford's Buick.

Above: By the 1960s, Grand National cars were built for racing, with roll bars, reinforced wheels, and engines that were suitably beefed up to handle 500-mile events on superspeedways. Yet this shot from 1961 of Jack Smith's No. 46 (1961 Pontiac), Friday Hassler's No. 96 (1960 Chevrolet), and Ralph Earnhardt's No. 6 (1961 Pontiac) shows that the cars retained their basic kinship with the cars sold at the local dealership. Note the horsepower numbers emblazoned on the hoods, a hallmark of this period. **Below:** By the 1970s, the emergence of big-money sponsorships had changed the look of the cars. Specially designed paint schemes featuring sponsor colors were the norm on all Winston Cup cars. And while the machines continued to evolve internally, the sheet metal was still more or less identical to cars on the street. This 1977 shot from Charlotte Motor Speedway shows Bobby Allison's No. 12 (AMC Matador) leading Cale Yarborough's No. 11 (Chevrolet Monte Carlo) and Dick Brooks' No. 90 (Ford Gran Torino). Note the short rear spoilers attached to the back of the trunk of each car.

Top: The cars are just beginning to look somewhat different than their road car cousins in this 1986 shot. Note the taller rear spoilers on the trunks and the low front spoiler on Bill Elliott's No. 9 Ford Thunderbird, which extends much farther down than on the production models. Yet Elliott's car is still distinctively different compared to Dale Earnhardt's No. 3 Chevrolet Monte Carlo. **Above:** The pretense of stock cars being based on production models more or less disappeared in the 1990s, as shown by this 1996 shot of Dale Earnhardt's No. 3 Chevrolet Monte Carlo leading Ernie Irvan's No. 28 Ford Thunderbird. Other than the somewhat distinguishing front grilles, the cars look more or less the same; however, what the machines lost in personality and similarity to their showroom brethren was more than made up for in the close and exciting racing that characterized the decade.

The Car of Today was another step in the direction toward making the cars safer and more evenly matched. As this shot from 2009 shows, a close look is required to find any features that set apart Kevin Harvick's No. 29 Chevrolet Impala SS from David Stremme's No. 12 Dodge Charger. (The front grilles and hood profiles are slightly dissimilar.) Although the latest NASCAR machine has been criticized by some drivers and fans, it has produced tight racing, along with an impressive ability to withstand punishment.

Liveries

In the early days, a car's livery, or paint scheme, usually included a number and sponsor displayed by way of white shoe polish and tape. But as the sport became more professional, teams naturally began to look toward certain colors to distinguish them from the rest, with Richard Petty's mix of medium blue and white "Petty Blue" color being the most famous example. By the 1970s, a car's livery was mostly determined by the sponsor's colors. Today's paint schemes are far more elaborate than ever; in fact, most of the colorful words and logos are not even paint at all: They are vinyl graphics created on a computer.

Above: This Oldsmobile's rather crude markings seem to indicate that the driver or owner did not employ the services of an experienced painter. The strips of tape could easily be removed, however. Wally Campbell drove this 1950 Oldsmobile to 52nd place (out of 75 cars!) at the 1950 Southern 500 at Darlington, earning $100 to bring back to Trenton, New Jersey. Note the leather belt keeping the driver's side door from swinging open during the race. **Right:** When team owner Carl Kiekhaefer decided to enter NASCAR, he didn't step in halfway. His fleet of Chrysler 300s dominated 1955 and 1956 and featured professionally painted numbers and the sponsorship markings of his company, Mercury Outboard Motors.

Left: Today's Sprint Cup car paint schemes are designed by professionals to ensure instant recognition for sponsors. This is Carl Edwards' Roush Fenway Racing Ford Fusion in August 2008. The teams change the cars' liveries each year—sometimes in subtle ways, sometimes with completely new looks—to keep the cars looking fresh.

Below: Today's Sprint Cup teams will often arrange one-off sponsorship deals to promote certain products or events. Here, Jeff Gordon's No. 24 Chevy Impala SS is wrapped in a special paint scheme at the October 2009 race at Lowe's Motor Speedway to mark the DVD release of the hit movie *Transformers: Revenge of the Fallen*.

Engines

In NASCAR, the drivers and cars are the visual show. But it's the 800-horsepower engines that provide the soundtrack, and it's the roar of the engines that stirs the soul of every NASCAR fan. In some ways, the NASCAR engine has not changed a great deal over the last several decades. While other race series have used or experimented with fuel injection, superchargers, and turbochargers and run engines with four, six, eight, ten, or even twelve cylinders, NASCAR has continued to run to the tried-and-true formula of carbureted V-8 engines. Today's, teams are strictly limited with what they can do to their powerplants, but some of the world's smartest engineers are working constantly to find that little extra edge.

This is a Petty Enterprises engine from the early 1960s. Chrysler's 427-cubic-inch big-block Hemi engines of the time were so powerful and dominant that NASCAR's founder, Bill France Sr., was forced to ban them from Grand National competition in 1965. Unfortunately, Petty Enterprises had already built a number of the engines, and the team was forced to abandon stock cars so they could run their engines on the drag strip. A year later, the engine was allowed to return with modifications.

Today's 358-cubic-inch engines are carefully engineered and constructed to endure 500 or more miles of brutal racing. Over the years, a combination of old-fashioned experience and engineering know-how has allowed teams to boost the maximum rpm from around 7,000 to 12,000 without catastrophic failure. Today's engine blocks and components are designed especially for racing, which helps minimize broken crankshafts, piston rods, and lifters.

Mechanics and Specialists

In the beginning, the NASCAR mechanic was often the same guy who drove the car to the track and then drove it in the race. But as the sport became more professional, owners began to form teams with one or a few dedicated mechanics, with the driver helping out wrenching as needed. Over time, the teams have grown and become far more structured. Today, Sprint Cup is more specialized than any other time in the sport's history. The top teams have annual budgets in the tens of millions of dollars, with staff employed to concentrate on specific areas of the race car. Chassis builders, fabricators, tire specialists, electronics specialists, and general mechanics work in unison to make certain every part of the car is race ready.

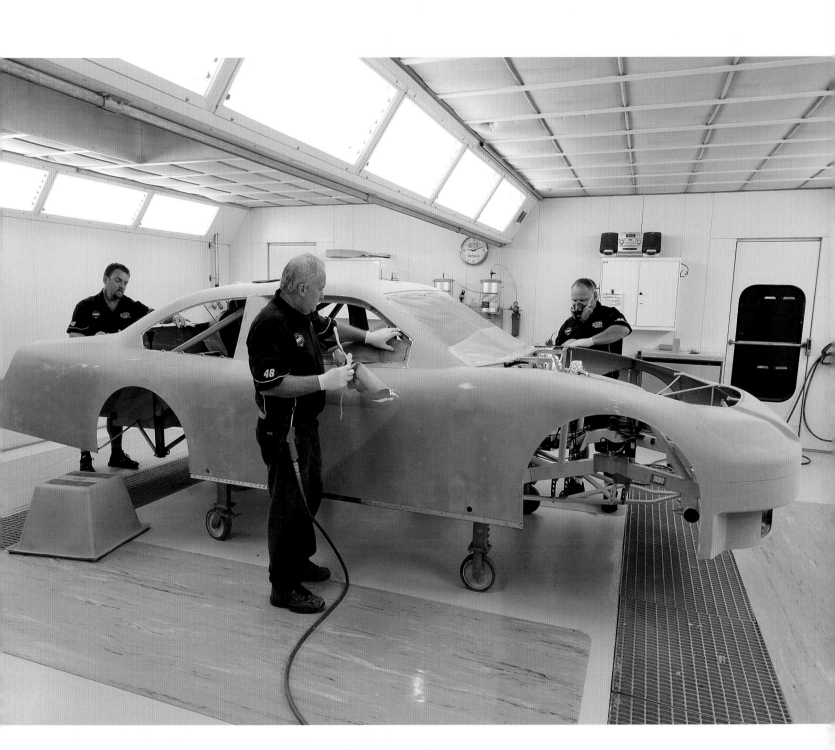

Above: Modern Sprint Cup team shops employ numerous highly skilled specialists. Here we see a team of painters at work on one of Jimmie Johnson's No. 48 Chevrolets at the Hendrick Motorsports race shop. The gray paint is a primer coat that goes straight onto the bodywork. The car's familiar dark blue and silver design will be added later.

Opposite: Legendary mechanic Herb Nab at work on an engine at the Holman-Moody shops in the early 1960s. Back in the day, the championship-winning crew chief didn't just work on the cars; he also participated in pit stops and any other tasks that were required of him.

Garages/Team Shops/Headquarters

An early NASCAR "race shop" usually consisted of a one-room wooden shed in the backyard behind the house. These were often no more than a 12-by-20-foot structure with a single light hanging from the rafters. The car was rolled out of the shed and worked on in the driveway, as there wasn't enough room inside for both car and mechanic. Some drivers who owned their own cars worked out of such small garages well into the 1970s.

In the early 1960s, manufacturer backing led to the creation of the first big shops, including the Chrysler-supported Petty Enterprises in Level Cross, North Carolina, and the Ford-backed Holman-Moody headquarters located in Charlotte. Over time, the successful and longstanding teams have grown to employ hundreds of people, and their headquarters have become attractions in themselves, with restaurants, gift shops, and guided tours for visitors.

Banjo Matthews stands at the center of his shop in Arden, North Carolina, during a busy day in the mid-1970s. Known as one of the sport's premier car builders, the former driver and team owner also handled extensive repairs for other teams.

A member of the Holman-Moody team works on an engine in the mid-1960s. Cameras were rarely allowed in the engine department of the shop.

Left: The Hendrick Motorsports shop is a state-of-the-art facility spread over several acres of carefully manicured landscapes.

Below: Here are No. 24 and No. 48 Chevrolets in various states of assembly inside the perfectly neat and orderly Hendrick facility.

The Office

The cockpit is the place where NASCAR drivers can forget about the many demands of their daily lives. It's the place where they can focus and do what they do best. Unfortunately, in years past the cockpit was also the place where some drivers lost their lives through violent crashes or deadly fires. In today's safety-conscious era, it seems hard to believe that the racers of yesteryear didn't even wear seatbelts, let alone fire-protection gear. (Many drivers felt they were better off being thrown out of the car than getting trapped in a burning wreck.)

The modern NASCAR Sprint Cup car was designed for maximum driver safety, with numerous innovations that have allowed drivers to walk away from even the most spectacular accidents. The sport will always have its dangers, but today's NASCAR driver knows that when he climbs into that cockpit, he can feel assured that the chances of climbing back out in one piece are better than they have ever been.

Above: This is Fred Lorenzen strapping on his helmet before a race in 1965. The view inside the cockpit of his Holman-Moody Ford shows that this car is a long way removed from the Strictly Stock family sedan, yet it is a far cry from today's car. Note the black electrical tape, limited roll bar padding, and no headrest behind Lorenzen's seat. **Right:** Jeff Burton is in the cockpit of his Richard Childress Racing Chevrolet before the start of the Sprint Cup event at New Hampshire Motor Speedway in June 2009. Note the carbon-fiber seat—which was custom-built to fit Burton's frame—with padding that wraps around Burton's head, torso, and legs to keep him safe in the event of side impacts. The steering wheel (removable to allow an easier exit from the car) is set close to the driver in order to save his or her arms from the fatigue that comes with reaching out to steer.

Chapter 4
The Tracks

NASCAR tracks then (above) and now (right): For the first 10 years of NASCAR's existence, the sands of Daytona Beach, Florida, offered drivers a great surface for racing—that is, if practice, qualifying, and the race could be completed before the ocean's tide came in during the late afternoon hours. Here Eddie Anderson is putting his No. 45 Nash through its paces on the Daytona Beach and Road Course in 1951. At the two-mile high-banked Michigan International Speedway, there is plenty of room for fans to have a comfortable view of the action on the track. Built in 1969, the facility has progressively grown over the past three decades and now accommodates more than 100,000 fans.

From the Dirt Tracks to the Superspeedways

During the formative years of NASCAR, races were run on oval dirt tracks cut into open fields and cow pastures with guardrails hastily installed. Despite these tight confines, drivers raced three wide into turns and it was not unusual for a driver to find himself off track and negotiating around patches of trees. The wheel men who could master the dirt were the ones who moved to the front of the field.

Stock car racing began to be accepted as a legitimate sport when asphalt short tracks and superspeedways replaced the small dirt bullrings. As time wore on and nationally known sponsors became involved in the sport, dirt tracks were more and more considered the way of the past and were taken completely off the NASCAR schedule. But those old bullrings will always be remembered as the foundation of decades of memorable races.

Herb Thomas gets his Hudson Hornet sideways around a dirt track in 1954. All that was needed to bring a dirt track to life was a vacant piece of land, some paint for poles, and grandstands full of interested fans.

Today's paved tracks are huge facilities with massive seating areas and high-banked turns. The 2.66-mile Talladega Superspeedway is the fastest of them all. The Alabama track opened in September 1969 amid controversy; drivers worried the tires would not hold up to the strain of speeds that surpassed 200 miles per hour. Over time, the tires were perfected, and today "The World's Fastest Race Track" hosts some of the closest, most exciting bumper-to-bumper racing on the NASCAR circuit.

Daytona International Speedway

The racing heritage of Daytona Beach stretches all the way back to the early 1900s when well-to-do "horseless carriage" enthusiasts attempted land speed records on the beach's hard-packed sands. The Beach and Road course opened in the 1930s and soon developed an enthusiastic following. Among the race's regular competitors was a certain Bill France Sr., who envisioned a purpose-built facility befitting Daytona's stature as a cornerstone of American racing.

After years of planning and local and state approvals, the Daytona International Speedway opened its gates in February 1959 to excited race fans from all over the country. Over the past five decades, the 2.5-mile track has been the site of NASCAR's biggest and most prestigious event, the Daytona 500. To be listed as a Daytona 500 winner makes a driver's career a success.

Right: The 500 isn't the only race held at the giant Daytona facility. The speedway also hosts the Daytona 200 motorcycle road race, as well as the prestigious 24 Hours of Daytona sports car race. And every July 4th weekend, the facility hosts a second NASCAR event, a night race currently called the Coke Zero 400. Holding races at night is a great way to avoid the sometimes brutal Florida heat experienced during summer days.

This shot from 1957 offers a great view of the long oval that made up the Daytona Beach and Road Course. At left is the beach with the Atlantic Ocean rolling in; at right is Highway A1A. That's Tim Flock sliding around the North Turn in the No. 15 Mercury.

Darlington Raceway

Patterned after the Indianapolis Motor Speedway, the famed Darlington Raceway was the brainchild of visionary Harold Brasington, a former race driver who turned his attention to construction and farming. Over time, the historic egg-shaped oval gained a reputation as one of the toughest tracks on the NASCAR circuit, its single racing groove and tight turns earning it the nicknames "The Lady in Black" and "The Track Too Tough to Tame." In recent years the track has been reconfigured: What was the front stretch is now the back stretch, and the turns have been renumbered accordingly. Seating has been increased to approximately 65,000 (the grandstand built in 1950 held 9,000). It remains one of the great venues in American racing.

An aerial shot of Darlington Raceway under construction shows its expansive original configuration. Built in 1950 over an old cotton field, the 1.366-mile speedway was designed in part to protect a small but productive minnow pond located just outside of the track's second turn. At right are the original turns one and two. Note the minnow pond just off the second turn behind the small clump of trees.

Darlington Raceway as it is today features lights and a weathered racing surface. The famous minnow pond is long gone. It remains a classic, one-of-a-kind track, and one of the most challenging ovals on the NASCAR schedule. Hitting the wall for the first time is a time-honored tradition for NASCAR rookies, all of whom will eventually earn their "Darlington stripe."
Photo courtesy Darlington Raceway.

Bristol Motor Speedway

When Carl Moore, Larry Carrier, and R. G. Pope came up with the idea of building a short track in the foothills of Tennessee, they had no idea it would become one of the most popular racing facilities in all of NASCAR. What began as a simple plan to bring stock car racing to the state turned out to be the tour's hottest ticket.

First opened in 1961 as Bristol International Speedway, the famed track has experienced spectacular growth over the decades. From its original 18,000-seat capacity, Bristol had grown to 71,000 by the time racing entrepreneur Bruton Smith purchased the facility in 1996. Smith changed the venue's name to Bristol Motor Speedway and immediately began renovations to redesign the track and increase capacity. The modern layout now seats 147,000 spectators, all eager to see Bristol's unique and intense form of short track racing.

Above: The Bristol Motor Speedway of today features many changes to its racing surface and grandstands. In 1992, the track was resurfaced from asphalt to concrete. Four years later, Bruton Smith bought the track for $26 million. In addition to doubling Bristol's seating capacity, Smith added 22 skyboxes and a spacious press box, all high above the racing surface. A Guinness World Record was set in August 2008 when the sell-out crowd completed the largest crowd wave in history.

Opposite: Bristol International Speedway was built on the site of a former dairy farm. The total cost of purchasing the land and building facility was approximately $600,000. The grounds covered about 100 acres and included parking for more than 12,000 cars. The half-mile track featured 60-foot-wide straightaways and 75-feet-wide turns with 22 degrees of banking. *Photo courtesy Bristol Motor Speedway*

Living Quarters

During NASCAR's early years, race fans often opened their homes to drivers and team members when they arrived in the area for the latest event. There were home-cooked dinners and clean sheets on beds, items considered luxuries since hotels were limited in many of the towns they visited. Over time, hotel chains began to spring up around racetracks, as their owners realized the benefit of offering thousands of fans (and teams) a temporary place to stay for the weekend.

As the sport has grown over the decades, the casual driver-fan interaction of the old days has more or less disappeared. The sheer number of fans requires today's tracks to provide secure areas for the teams to stay in. By the early 1990s, drivers began to enjoy the convenience of having motor homes on site at the tracks. These homes on wheels give drivers easy access to the garage areas and a place for them to relax with their families during down times.

While sitting in the family van, seven-time NASCAR champion Richard Petty eagerly checks out a cake and other food items prepared by his wife, Lynda, before the start of a race in 1986. Drivers and their families of that era used local hotels in the area.

The modern NASCAR driver motorhome features comfortable beds, a bathroom with shower, flat-screen TVs with satellite reception, and a fully functional galley. Here Kurt (left) and Kyle Busch talk racing in Kyle's bachelor pad on wheels. Note the wood panel stowaway cabinets and vase with flower on the table.

Track Safety

Racing always has been and always will be a dangerous sport. What has changed between the old days and today is what is considered an acceptable level of risk. Not much thought was given to safety in NASCAR's early years. Little was done to the cars or tracks to protect drivers or spectators; the inevitable result was that many drivers—and even some fans—paid the ultimate price. At the time, this was considered part and parcel of the racing experience—"you knew what you were getting into."

Thankfully, that attitude has changed. Over the decades, NASCAR officials have worked tirelessly to ensure the safety of fans while greatly reducing the risk of injury or death for drivers. Today's NASCAR tracks are built and maintained to rigorous safety standards, with new innovations coming virtually every year. The result of all of these efforts is that racing-related injuries

Track safety has come a long way from the old dirt tracks, when rickety wooden fences—if anything—were all that stood between the fans and speeding cars, and a trackside clump of trees might be the last thing a driver sees after making a fatal mistake at top speed.

are rare, fatalities even more so. Yet safety is a moving target, and NASCAR continues to strive to make its tracks as safe as they can be.

Modern tracks, such as New Hampshire Motor Speedway, keep fans safe with tall chain-link fencing anchored in concrete. These fences are built to withstand the impact of a flying stock car without collapsing. The multilayered wall that Patrick Carpentier has hit is a Steel and Foam Energy Reduction (SAFER) barrier, which is designed to absorb some of the force of an impact, protecting the driver from injury.

Standard highway guardrails were the norm at superspeedways in the early 1960s. They were generally effective in keeping the cars on track in normal situations, but the consequences could be grim when they failed. At the 1961 World 600 at Charlotte Motor Speedway, Reds Kagle lost one of his legs when he slammed into the guardrail with such violence that it severed the barrier. His car was impaled by the guardrail.

At bottom left of this photo is an inside view of the SAFER barrier. The outer wall is actually a series of square steel tubes welded together. The arrow-shaped elements are stacks of thick foam. When a car makes a hard impact, the system absorbs much of the energy, and the foam pieces will often become dislodged. All of today's NASCAR tracks have SAFER barriers along outside turns and on some inside walls.

Above: This shot of the Daytona pit road shows a much safer environment for teams and officials. The speedway's tri-oval layout places pit road far away from the racetrack. Pit lane itself is also considerably wider—with clearly marked stalls for each car.

Opposite: The pit lanes are another area where great strides have been made in regards to safety. In this 1950 shot at Darlington, cars fly past the open pit area where hundreds of crew members stand close by. The crew working on the car in the foreground is mere inches from race traffic. With no wall separating the pits and track, an out-of-control car veering into the pits would likely have resulted in dozens of injuries—or worse.

Trackside Stables

The sound is music to the ears of any NASCAR fan: The roar of the 800-horsepower thoroughbred engines echoing around the speedway. The hardcore fans arrive early—long before the first practice session or race—just to hear those first exhaust notes, to take in those early morning thunderclaps coming from the infield garages. For some, this is what NASCAR is all about: the sound of one of the greatest toys ever invented by mankind— the internal combustion engine.

The garage area at a NASCAR track is like the locker room at a sports stadium or the backstage area at a music arena. It's where the stars of the show make last-minute preparations, work themselves up into a frenzy before hitting the stage, and return to regroup when the show is over. Compared to yesteryear, today's trackside stables are much larger and more spacious, but they remain the place to find— and hear—the stars of the NASCAR show.

It's March 30, 1962, and dozens of cars sit packed tightly together, idling under the fluorescent lights of the Atlanta Motor Speedway garage area during a rainout of the Grand National event.

The state-of-the-art Las Vegas Motor Speedway features the Neon Garage, a complex that allows fans an unprecedented view of the garage area.

Hall of Fame crew chief Herb Nab works on the Junior Johnson–owned Chevrolet driven by Cale Yarborough in 1973. Back then, the garage areas resembled shop stalls with few accessories other than electrical outlets and wooden workbenches.

Modern garage areas have plenty of room for teams to stow their tools and equipment for the race weekend. Even with all that space, an engine change requires the car to be rolled outdoors. Here the Joe Gibbs Racing crew members perform an engine swap on Kyle Busch's No. 18 Toyota Camry.

Chapter 5

Setting the Stage

NASCAR transporters then (above) and now (opposite): During the 1981 Winston Cup season, a sign painter puts the final touches on the rear door of the team transporter of Darrell Waltrip's Junior Johnson—owned Buicks. Kyle Busch's M&M's-sponsored truck is nothing less than a rolling advertising billboard. Like the cars they carry, today's transporters feature vivid, computer-generated vinyl graphics.

Haulers

Years ago, getting race cars to the track required nothing more than a truck and trailer. Today's transporters are virtual rolling shops, carrying the tools and parts needed to solve any mechanical problem that might be encountered during a race weekend, including a spare engine, chassis components, jack stands, tape rolls, cutting tools, shocks, a welder, extra sheet metal, and complete rear end housing. In addition, today's haulers also carry a spare race car to each event.

Once unloaded, the transporter serves as a work area with computers and a television that the crew uses to monitor qualifying and practice speeds. It's also a place for the driver and crew chief to meet to discuss changes that need to be made to the car for better handling and speed.

Right: Jimmie Johnson watches his No. 48 car being unloaded from the transporter. Two Sprint Cup cars usually make the trip to the track with one deemed primary and the other secondary. The primary car is rolled out of the transporter for use during the weekend. Should a crash occur and heavily damage the car, the secondary car is taken out and pressed into service. Both cars are prepared as identically as possible in case that happens.

Above: Fred Lorenzen's Ford Fairlane is loaded and ready for the trip from Junior Johnson's shop in North Carolina to Atlanta Motor Speedway. Unlike modern race machines, the car will be exposed to the elements as it rides along the highway, no doubt to the delight of race fans who happen to see it motoring past. This photo was taken in 1966 and already demonstrates how much the sport had grown from the Strictly Stock days when racers drove their cars to the track.

Consultation

In today's NASCAR, it's no longer enough to just have a fast driver and a fast car. Every Sprint Cup driver is fast, and just about any Sprint Cup car can be a challenger on any given day. In many ways, it's communication that separates the great from the merely good. The best wheelmen have a feel for their cars and can communicate what they're doing to their crew chiefs in order to make the adjustments needed to get the maximum performance for qualifying and the best results on race day.

Then, as now, practice sessions are a crucial part of any weekend. They are the time to iron out any wrinkles, to methodically work through different setup scenarios, and to find the car's "sweet spot" that allows the driver to run at the front. Practice sessions were even more vital during the sport's earlier days, when technology to make mid-race chassis adjustments had not yet been introduced into the sport. The key to success has always been good communication.

Two of America's greatest racing legends, Smokey Yunick and a very young Mario Andretti, converse prior to the start of the 1966 Daytona 500. Both men enjoyed success in Indy car racing as well as stock cars. Andretti would crash his Chevrolet out of NASCAR's biggest event in 1966 before going on to win the race for Holman-Moody a year later.

Greg Zipadelli and Joey Logano make up a modern example of the wise and successful crew chief working with a young and highly talented driver. Here the two discuss chassis changes, with Zipadelli employing the hand gestures that make up the universal language understood by all race drivers. Zipadelli's movements suggest that the Joe Gibbs Racing No. 20 Home Depot car is struggling with some tightness, or push, into the turns.

The Rollout

This is one moment of the race weekend that hasn't changed much over the decades. Aside from winning the race, one of the proudest moments for any team is when the car is rolled out onto the starting grid. Doing so means everything that could possibly be done to the car has been completed. Practice and qualifying are done, checklists have been scanned, and all pieces on the car have been double-checked. There is simply nothing left to do other than push the car into place in front of thousands of cheering fans. The next time the crew touches the car will be during pit stops, and, if all goes well, when it rolls into victory lane.

Richard Petty's crew hustles his trademark red-and-blue No. 43 STP Dodge Charger down the Darlington pit road toward its starting position prior to a race in 1976. Petty campaigned Dodges and Chryslers for much of his 32-year career.

Although the graphics will change from time to time depending upon sponsorship agreements, the race cars of today are never hard to identify. The Joe Gibbs Racing crew pushes Kyle Busch's colorful Toyota Camry down pit road at Charlotte Motor Speedway in May 2009.

Pre-Race Ceremonies

Nothing highlights NASCAR's growth from a humble-but-ambitious race series to a season-long tour of events like today's pre-race ceremonies. In the 1950s and 1960s the pre-race festivities largely consisted of gathering the competitors at the start-finish line where the announcer conducted brief pre-race interviews to be heard on the radio and over the speedway's public address system. Today's pre-race shows are designed to whip up the fans into a frenzy of excitement. Makeshift stages are pulled to the start-finish line on the front stretch and quickly assembled. Equipped with bright lights, eye-catching graphics, and even pods that shoot colorful fireworks, these stages host live music performed by big ticket entertainers and are the place where drivers, team owners, track officials, and dignitaries are interviewed.

In keeping with NASCAR tradition, the pre-race ceremonies conclude with a prayer and a performance of "The Star-Spangled Banner," with the U.S. military stamping a sonic exclamation point over the proceedings with a perfectly timed fighter jet flyover at the conclusion. The crowd, the drivers, the teams, the officials, and the media are pumped up and ready for four hours of NASCAR-style excitement. Moments later, the drivers climb into their cars. Over the public address system, the famous command is given: "Gentlemen, start your engines!" All the hours of work, preparation, and anticipation are about to be put to the test. The race is about to begin. . . .

Edward Glenn "Fireball" Roberts acknowledges the crowd during driver introductions before the 1960 Rebel 300 at Darlington. Roberts was one of the most popular drivers of his era and his untimely death following a crash and fire in 1964 was a major blow to the sport.

Today's drivers aren't just introduced: They are literally paraded before the crowd, as Mark Martin demonstrates before the August 2009 race at Bristol. This was no typical driver parade for Martin, though, as the huge crowd surprised him with a "card trick" celebrating the veteran racer's 1,000th career NASCAR start.

Above: Today, all 36 races of the NASCAR Sprint Cup season are aired live on a major broadcast or cable network. Here former NASCAR-driver-turned-broadcaster Phil Parsons interviews Dale Earnhardt Jr. before the race at Las Vegas in March 2008. Today, pre-race interviews take place not only on pit lane, but even while the drivers are in the car running the pace laps prior to the green flag.

Opposite: Pre-race interviews have been a part of the pre-race ritual ever since radio, and later television, began covering the sport. Here Richard Petty (left) prepares to talk with highly respected ABC Sports commentator Chris Economaki prior to the start of the 1967 Daytona 500. At that time the network usually aired segments of tape-delayed races during its Saturday afternoon *Wide World of Sports* telecasts.

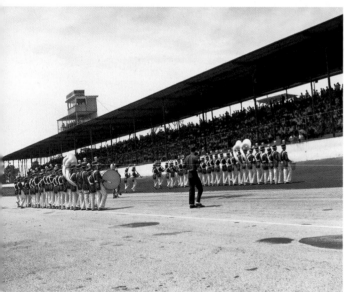

Top: This is the calm before the storm. The pre-race prayer is a tradition that runs back to the first NASCAR event more than 60 years ago. **Right:** The modern version is organized with efficiency on par with a military parade. **Above:** Years ago, the featured musical guest was usually the local high school marching band. Today's events draw some of the top acts from various forms of entertainment. **Opposite top:** The national anthem offers a few final moments for the drivers to be with their families before the race gets underway. **Opposite bottom:** The moment reaches a crescendo with a flyover by fighter jets. In this case, it's the six F-16 Fighting Falcons that make up the U.S. Air Force's Thunderbirds demonstration team.

Chapter 6
Let's Go Racin'!

Whether it's the 1969 Daytona 500 (below) or the 2005 Banquet 400 at Kansas Speedway (right), every NASCAR race starts with a series of laps behind the pace car. These are essentially warm-up laps, run at 30 to 80 miles per hour (depending on the track), allowing engines and tires to get up to temperature. They also give the drivers a few moments to prepare themselves mentally for the job at hand. One difference between the pace laps of today and yesterday: The drivers of yesteryear were alone with their thoughts and the rumbling of their engines. Today's drivers are connected to their crew chiefs and spotters via two-way radio.

Green Flag!

In football, basketball, and hockey, it's a referee's whistle. In baseball, it's the umpire's call to, "Play ball!" In stock car racing—and in nearly every other form of motorsports—the competition begins with the wave of the green flag. It's the time-honored tradition that gets the 43-car field up to speed and down to business.

This wrinkled old photo has seen better days; maybe it's too rough around the edges to even use in a book. But it's a perfect shot of a moment in time long past. The race starter (at right) is standing inside the track waving the green flag to begin a modified race in the early 1950s. The track looks as if it was cut out of a vacant field. Note the barn on the hill in the distance.

Right: Today, the act of waving the green flag is still the same, but it's done from a flag stand raised high above the track where the whole field can see. At today's Sprint Cup races, the honor of starting the race is usually given to a celebrity, dignitary, or other honored person. The thrill of standing just a few feet above a roaring stampede of stock cars as they come up to speed is an experience they will remember for a lifetime.

Rubbin' Is Racin'

To a driver, track position is everything. For hundreds of laps throughout a given race, drivers work hard to find any advantage possible. At times, that advantage comes with the help of the car beside them when they "lean on" a fellow competitor to help get through a turn. Other times, it's two drivers going for the same piece of real estate. The result is sheet metal grinding together and decals and sponsor markings taking the brunt of the impact. To the race fans in the stands, rubbing fenders or sides with another driver on the short tracks serves as something of a badge of honor. It means their favorite driver has no reservations about fighting and clawing for position. In the end, it may mean the difference between winning and losing.

With dirt flying and fans just a few feet from the action, Buck Baker (No. 300), Junior Johnson (No. 55), and Ralph Moody (No. 12) battle for position around a lapped car during a Strictly Stock race at Asheville-Weaverville Speedway on July 1, 1956. In the end, Lee Petty would take the win in a Dodge.

Close racing is one thing that will never change in NASCAR, especially on short tracks such as Richmond International Raceway, shown here. NASCAR's modern racing machines are built to withstand the bumping and banging that goes along with these door-to-door, wheel-to-wheel slugfests without any significant loss in performance. Shown here in the heat of battle are Jeff Burton (No. 31), Casey Mears (No. 07), and Ryan Newman (No. 39) in September 2009.

Right: By the late 1980s, Winston Cup cars were reaching speeds of well over 200 miles per hour at superspeedways such as Daytona and Talladega. The dangers of that kind of velocity became all too apparent when Bobby Allison blew a tire at Talladega, causing his car to spin, fly through the air, and slam into the catch fencing, injuring several spectators. To slow the cars down on the big tracks, NASCAR mandated that cars run with carburetor restrictor plates. The plates have brought the speeds down to a more manageable 190 miles per hour, but they also make the cars very equal, resulting in the vehicles bunching together in large packs. This can make for exciting, nail-biting racing, but so many cars traveling so close together at the same speeds almost inevitably leads to multi-car accidents. Here Kyle Busch leads the six-wide (!) field at the April 2009 Talladega Sprint Cup race

Above: The larger ovals let drivers keep the pedal to the floor for most—sometimes all—of the lap. This allows the cars to string out a bit, especially on long green flag runs. But thanks to the wonders of the draft—the vacuum effect created by a leading car punching a hole in the air, helping to carry the trailing cars along—the leader can never feel too safe. Especially when a caution can come out at any time to bunch up the field again. Here Cale Yarborough leads the pack on his way to victory at the 1977 Daytona 500.

Impact!

Bill France's original vision of Strictly Stock meant just that: stock machines right off the dealership lot. For a few hundred bucks, just about any wannabe race driver could try his hand at wheeling his car on dirt. More often than not, however, those dreams of glory turned upside down after a blown tire or broken tie-rod sent the family sedan tumbling. While the pastime has never been safe, the dangers were kept in check back then by the fact that the Strictly Stock cars were relatively slow by today's standards.

As the wreckage piled up, the first order of business was to find a way to reinforce the somewhat flimsy tops of the cars so they wouldn't collapse on the driver. This was done with roll bars installed inside the cars to reinforce the tops. These and other safety improvements meant the cars were no longer Strictly Stock, but at least they weren't death traps.

Through the decades, NASCAR stock cars have steadily evolved, reaching speeds that would have seemed like science fiction to the drivers of old. Safety has steadily evolved along with the speeds, sometimes from a proactive approach, sometimes through tragedy. Today's Sprint Cup machines are designed with the most up-to-date safety features available. Recent years have witnessed horrific-looking rollover crashes, with cars coming to rest in mangled heaps after repeated mid-air somersaults. Yet drivers have continued to emerge from the wreckage virtually unscathed, thanks to more than 60 years of safety innovation. Here's hoping the trend continues for another 60 years.

Below: Johnny Beauchamp's No. 73 takes a ride over the guardrail during the qualifying race for the 1961 Daytona 500. Beauchamp had locked up with Lee Petty, sending both over the guardrail. Petty was severely injured in the crash and was forced to end his racing career.

Joey Logano (No. 20 Toyota) takes to the air after tangling with Reed Sorenson (No. 43 Dodge), Robby Gordon (No. 7 Toyota), and Martin Truex Jr. (No. 1 Chevrolet) at Dover International Speedway in September 2009. Logano walked away uninjured despite rolling his Joe Gibbs Racing Toyota Camry several times.

What at first looked to be a tragedy turned out to be a miracle. Legendary Darlington Raceway photographer Tom Kirkland captured this incredible sequence at the 1958 Southern 500. Jack Smith loses control of his Chevrolet, which climbs the guardrail and disappears over the side of the track into the parking lot below. The final shot in the sequence shows the mangled car at rest surrounded by a crowd of onlookers. (Note the intrepid photographer standing in the scaffolding.) Miraculously, the car did not land on anyone, and Smith suffered only minor injuries.

Our own legendary NASCAR photographer, Nigel Kinrade, was in the right place at the right time when Ryan Newman's Penske Racing Dodge took flight at the 2003 Daytona 500. Newman's machine became airborne after hitting the wall and veering into the infield. The car dug into the grass, allowing air to get underneath, which sent the car flying and rolling in a heap of mangled parts. The Dodge's roll cage protected Newman, who crawled out of the car after suffering only minor injuries.

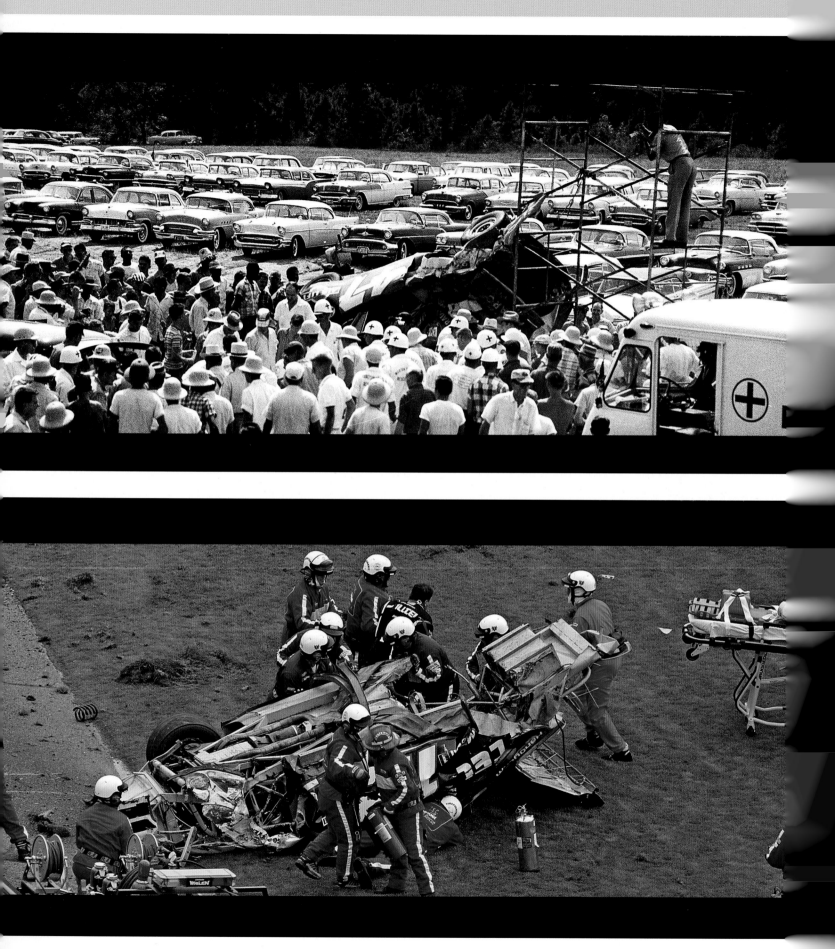

Two years after Jack Smith's off-track excursion, Johnny Allen did the same during the 1960 Rebel 300 at Darlington. This wreck could have been a tragedy, as Allen's car tore through the scorer's stand (the scaffolding that can be seen at left) on its way off the track. Track photographer Tom Kirkland explained what happened in his book *Darlington International Raceway 1950–1967:* "Fortunately, the sun was shining in the end that the car hit. So, all the scorers who had been in that section had moved down to the shady end. No one was sitting where the scorer's stand crumpled. And no one was hurt. Johnny Allen walked away."

Communication

For decades, pit-to-driver communication was mostly a one-way street and consisted of a simple hand-held chalkboard that conveyed instructions about when to pit and queried the driver on car performance for upcoming pit stop adjustments. The benefits of two-way radio communication were obvious from the start, but it took several decades for the technology to catch up to the idea. Jack Smith tried equipping his car with an old ham radio at the 1960 World 600 at Charlotte Motor Speedway, but the tubes jostled loose under all the high-speed vibrations. In 1973 Bobby Allison modified a citizens' band (CB) radio with speakers inside his helmet, but reception was spotty. By the 1980s, the sport had worked out most of the bugs, and today's teams rely heavily on two-way communication between the driver, the pits, and the spotters watching the action from high above. Radios have added an extra element for the media and fans, who get to listen in on conversations during the race.

Delano Wood of the Wood Brothers team asks David Pearson a question during a race at North Carolina Motor Speedway in 1978. Drivers also used hand signals to communicate with the pits. For example, when the car was loose and on the edge of spinning out of control, drivers would pat the top of the car. When it was tight and hard to steer, they would touch the top of the driver's door.

The headset worn by crew chief Pat Tryson allows him to communicate with his driver, his spotter, the team garage, and NASCAR officials. The earpieces also protect the crew members' ears from the deafening roar of 40-plus 800-horsepower race engines.

Pit Stops

Few elements of a NASCAR race demonstrate the sport's evolution from an amateur pastime to a professional world-class sport like pit stops. Pit stops weren't even part of the equation in the early days, as the typical short track event was limited to about one hundred miles. But speedways allowed the cars to run significantly longer distances, requiring stops for refueling, tire changes, and mechanical adjustments.

The pit stops of the 1950s were measured in minutes, not seconds. Jacks were heavy and cumbersome, tires were hard to manage, and in-race handling adjustments were pretty much unheard of. But racing is always about going faster than the other guy, and over timve the sport's innovators came up with more and more ways to shave time off their pit stops. For example, crewmen struggled to get lugs on wheel studs until the mid-1960s, when the Wood Brothers began gluing the lugs straight on to the rims, saving precious seconds, if not minutes, with each tire change. Today, NASCAR's dedicated pit crews can change four tires, refuel, and make chassis adjustments in less than 13 seconds.

No one appears to be in too big of a hurry as they work on Dick Rathmann's Hudson Hornet during a race at Darlington in 1952. The number of people standing around apparently just observing the action would be unheard of in a modern NASCAR race, where access to the pit lane is strictly limited for safety and competition reasons. Note the makeshift debris screen over the grille and what looks to be a bungee-cord keeping the hood in check. Rathmann would go on to win the race.

Your eyes are not deceiving you. Yes, that is Richard Petty, in his driver's suit and famous cowboy boots, beating the tar out of his Plymouth with a hammer. This happened during a pit stop at the 1968 Daytona 500; Petty was attempting an on-the-fly repair to the car's vinyl roof, which was popping up and slowing down his car.

Today's pit stops are perfectly choreographed down to the split second and practiced thousands of times by crew members. Only six people are allowed over the wall at any time during the race, and yet Juan Pablo Montoya's Earnhardt Ganassi Racing team changed four tires and refueled his Chevrolet in less than 14 seconds during this stop at Dover International Speedway in May 2009. Note the two long poles appearing out of the right side of the photo: one for removing debris from the grille and another delivering liquid to Montoya.

Above: NASCAR's safety improvements haven't just aided drivers and spectators, they have also helped protect crewmembers, as this shot taken at Kansas Speedway in 2009 shows Scott Speed's Red Bull Racing crew decked out in protective fire suits with helmets. The two gas men (each carrying a 10-gallon can) also wear aprons to keep the fuel from making contact with their bodies. The red box just visible in front of the man behind the car is the catch can, a container that catches any excess fuel to keep it from spilling on the car or ground.

Opposite: Good thing no one was smoking during this late-1960s pit stop at North Carolina Motor Speedway. Things don't look to be going very smoothly for this gas man; much of what he is pouring into the tank appears to be leaking out of the back of the car. Note the complete lack of any safety clothing or gear. Not only was this situation one spark away from a disaster, the high-octane fuel spilling on the crewman no doubt caused him skin irritation.

Bringing It Home

Every driver starts a race looking to take the checkered flag. But with 42 other competitors gunning for the same goal, even the best drivers and teams have the odds stacked against them. As seven-time champion Richard Petty, the most successful driver in all of NASCAR history, has often pointed out, he started 1,184 races in his career but won *only* 200 of them. In those remaining 984 races, Petty battled for points, and the points gained in those non-winning races were the foundation for his seven titles. Every completed lap can count toward points—even finishing 42nd means more than finishing 43rd. This is why teams will go to incredible lengths to patch up a crippled car and throw it back out on the track, even if the chance to win the race disappeared hours earlier in a puff of smoke or a pile of mangled sheet metal. A point gained here or there may make all the difference in the final tally.

Benny Parsons' 1973 championship season was proof that strong and consistent points finishes can pay off in the end. Parsons took the title despite winning just one race. David Pearson won 11 but ran only a limited schedule, while Richard Petty won 6 and Cale Yarborough won 4. Parsons' 19 top-10 finishes would beat them all, but only just. After crashing early on during the last race of the season, Parsons' crew (with help from some other teams) pieced back together his shattered Chevrolet and sent it back out on the track to record enough laps to clinch the title.

Jimmie Johnson's quest for a historic fourth straight title took a hit during the third-to-last race of the season at Texas Motor Speedway. Johnson got caught up in a wreck that left the No. 48 Chevrolet heavily damaged. No one would have blamed the team for sitting out the rest of the race, but the crew went to work and sent the car back out with a brand-new nose (among other things). Johnson finished in 38th—128 laps behind the winner—and lost more than 100 points off his lead in the championship. It could have been far worse, and those few precious points came in handy at the end of the season.

Checkered Flag

Some traditions should never change and probably never will. The checkered flag has become a universal symbol of racing, better known than even the green flag. For generations, every driver dreams of the moment of being at the front when that black-and-white flag is waved. The thrill of victory is what every true competitor fights for, and that moment of glory makes all the sacrifice that came before seem worthwhile.

Dick Rathmann, Hudson Hornet, Darlington Raceway, 1952.

Ned Jarrett, Ford Galaxie, Asheville-Weaverville (North Carolina) Speedway, 1964.

Brian Vickers, Red Bull Racing Toyota Camry, Michigan International Speedway, 2009.

Jimmie Johnson, Hendrick Motorsports Chevrolet Impala SS, Martinsville Speedway, 2009.

Victory Lap

In the early days, victory laps were actually extra trips around the speedway to make certain the fans were able to complete their old-fashioned scorecards that determined position and final finishing order. They were also a way for the driver and fans to revel in the moment of success. Over the years, victory celebrations have become much more elaborate and make for a fitting encore to an exciting show.

"Johnny Reb" was a fixture at Darlington Raceway throughout the 1960s. Here he takes his traditional victory lap ride on the hood of Richard Petty's winning Plymouth at the conclusion of the 1967 Southern 500. Ironically, the man who played the fictional character for most of those years was not a Southerner at all: His name was Bob van Witzenburg, and he was born and raised in Holland before coming to the United States as a high school exchange student. Van Witzenburg was recruited for the role from his job working for the local radio station. Petty won 27 of 46 races as well as the NASCAR championship that season.

Today, no NASCAR victory lap is complete until the driver performs the traditional burnout. Here Jimmie Johnson shows how it's done after notching another victory at Auto Club Speedway in Fontana, California, in 2009. Note the checkered flag in Johnson's hand. Grabbing the flag from the official to carry along on the victory lap is another modern-day NASCAR tradition.

No driver celebrates a victory like Carl Edwards. The ultra-athletic Roush driver's signature victory backflip is famous all over the world. He demonstrates it here after taking the win at Texas Motor Speedway in 2008. Kids: Don't try this at home.

Victory Lane

They say everybody loves a winner, and NASCAR is no exception. Victory Lane has always been a crowded place after a race; there's never a shortage of people who want to be there to bask in a driver's glory. As you might expect, NASCAR victory lane celebrations have become far more elaborate and sophisticated over the years, evolving from a brief and casual trophy presentation to the highly choreographed and scripted media shows of today.

Here's a sight you certainly won't see in Victory Lane today: This is the legendary Fonty Flock enjoying a smoke after snagging the winner's trophy at the Raleigh 300 at Southland Speedway (as Raleigh Speedway was known at the time) in 1953. Flock's shorts no doubt kept him cool inside the car, but they wouldn't have been much help if he'd dropped his cigarette in his lap during the race.

Buddy Baker looks to be struggling to catch his breath as he climbs on top of his Petty Enterprises Dodge in victory lane after winning the World 600 at Charlotte Motor Speedway in May 1972. The man at left appears about to hand Baker a Pepsi, which he will no doubt appreciate, having just finished racing for 4 hours and 13 minutes at an average speed of 142 miles per hour.

Left: Today's victory lane celebrations are designed to deliver maximum exposure for sponsors. Here Mark Martin (somewhat dwarfed behind the podium and trophy) delivered the goods for sponsors Kellogg's and Car Quest at Phoenix International Raceway in April 2009. The entire crew is brought to the stage to celebrate and to have their photos taken. The woman in the front row, fourth from right, is Miss Sprint Cup, Monica Palumbo, who, along with fellow Miss Sprint Cup Anne-Marie Rhodes, represents the series sponsor at all events. **Above:** Mark Martin raises the trophy in triumph. Note that he has changed his hat from the other picture. Victory lane celebrations include a sequence of hat changes to make sure every sponsor's hat and logo is photographed.

Post-Race Interviews

Years ago, even the race winner's media duties didn't go much further than brief interviews for radio (possibly TV) and offering some commentary for NASCAR beat reporters. For today's NASCAR driver, the job doesn't end with the checkered flag. Win or lose, drivers are expected to be available to the media immediately after the race. In fact, drivers will often have to face TV cameras and microphones before they have even climbed out of their cars. In the case of a driver who experienced some controversy during the race, the media's goal is to catch the driver in the heat of the moment, before he or she has a chance to simmer down, in hopes the driver says something newsworthy. For the fiercely competitive racers who make up NASCAR's Sprint Cup Series, keeping your temper under control after the race can sometimes be a bigger challenge than keeping your car under control during the race.

Chris Economaki interviews Junior Johnson after taking the checkered flag at the 1962 Southern 500. Johnson's mood would sour considerably a few hours later when it was determined a scoring error had been made and that Larry Frank was the true winner of the race.

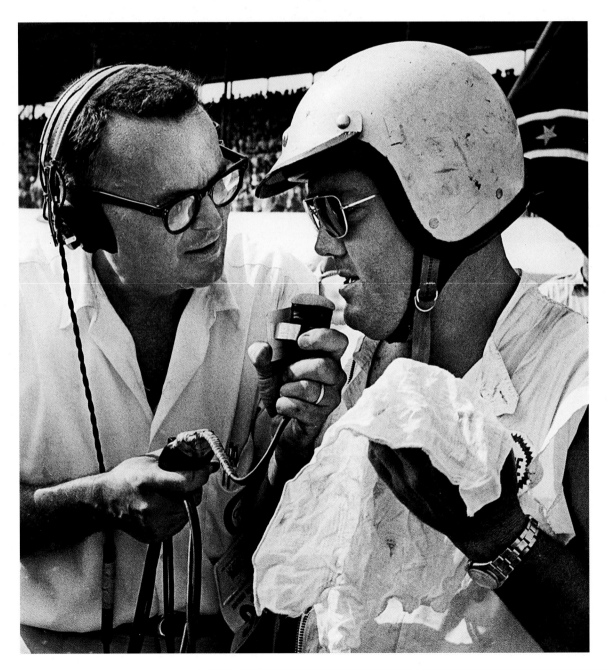

Tony Stewart (left) and Stewart-Haas teammate Ryan Newman look tired but relatively happy as they hold court for reporters following the 2009 Southern 500 at Darlington. Stewart is legendary for his willingness to speak his mind and not mince words; many fellow drivers (and reporters) have felt his wrath over the years. The two have reason to be cheerful here, though, as they finished a respective third and fourth in the race.

War Wounds

Anyone who doesn't think NASCAR drivers are true athletes should try putting on several layers of clothing and a full-face helmet, climb into a car that is 100 degrees or hotter inside, and spend four hours driving at lethal speeds surrounded by dozens of other cars. The sport's grueling nature is sometimes overlooked, but 500 miles is a long trip, especially in the heat of summer. The majority of today's drivers take their conditioning seriously and work with personal trainers and nutritionists to keep themselves in peak condition. This sort of approach would have seemed ridiculous to the many heavy-smoking, hard-drinking drivers of yesteryear, but it's just another way to gain an advantage over your competitors.

An exhausted Cale Yarborough takes some oxygen as he sits beside his Wood Brothers Ford after a race in 1968.

Frank Warren gets a smile from his daughter as he cools his feet following a very hot race at Talladega Superspeedway in 1977.

Dave Marcis displays the wounds suffered trying to control an ill-handling Dodge at the 1971 Southern 500 at Darlington. The big cars raced in the 1970s didn't have power steering. Today's drivers are required to wear fireproof gloves.

David Stremme looks drained after 400 miles of restrictor plate racing at the Coke Zero 400 at Daytona. Drivers can lose as much as 10 pounds in water weight over the course of a hot race, despite today's cars being equipped with "cool box" systems that circulate (relatively) cool air through their helmets.

Packing Up

The show is over and the fans have gone home, but the work is far from done. For the crewmembers, it's time to pack up everything and hit the road for a long drive back to team headquarters or to the next track on the schedule. In the early days of the sport, the owner, crew chief, and driver did a lot of the work themselves. Today, once the drivers finish debriefing with their teams, they can head to the airport with their families and hop a plane—maybe their own plane—home. The schedule can take its toll on NASCAR's unsung heroes, but it's a price these people happily pay to be a part of the sport they love.

Right: Michael Waltrip's battered Toyota (center) is loaded into the transporter, while the Ford Fusions of Erik Darnell (left) and Paul Menard do the same. The sun appears to be beginning its slow descent toward the horizon at Phoenix International Raceway. A long drive to team headquarters in North Carolina lies ahead.

One of the famed Carl Kiekhaefer–owned Chryslers is loaded into the truck after a crash earlier in the day. The covered transporter truck was unusual for its time and a sign of the level of expense and professionalism Kiekhaefer invested during his brief time in the sport.

Photo Acknowledgments

All contemporary images by Nigel Kinrade.
All historical images, Smyle Media:

Don Hunter Collection
Back cover (top left, bottom right), pages 1, 3 (top),
7–12, 14, 16–18, 20, 22, 24, 28–30, 32, 34 (top), 38, 44, 46,
48, 51, 56, 61 (bottom), 62, 64 (bottom), 66, 68, 70, 72,
78, 84, 86, 90–92, 94, 96, 98, 102, 106, 108, 110, 112, 122,
124 (bottom), 126, 128, 130, 132, 135, 138, 140, 141.

Tom Kirkland Archive
Pages 2 (top), 6, 26, 32, 34 (bottom), 36, 40, 42, 50,
52, 55, 58, 60, 61 (top), 64 (top), 74, 76, 80, 87, 88, 100,
104, 114, 116–121, 124 (top), 130, 134, 142.

Index